Foreword

I dedicate this book to the three women who have had the most influence on my life. The first person is my wife who I love more than life itself. Rachel, you are prized and loved. You are like the Rachel of the Holy Bible, a wife that is worth the wait. A wife that is worth the sacrifice and waiting for! The second person I dedicate this book to is my beloved mother who has left a mark on my life in the greatest way! I love you, mom! The last person I dedicate this book to is my great aunt Eva. May you rest in peace! I thank you for fighting for my right to live. This book is here because thirty-eight years ago you denied the abortionists the right to my life! You fought for my right to live! So this book is a monument to you!

Contents

What Came Before

    The Stock I Come From

    The Principle of the Streetlight

    The Bello's

    My Best Friend Rick

    Latter Day Saint

    Seaman Green

    Elder Green

    Disability

    I Need A Angel

    How to Overcome

Emotional Control

The Book on the Exes

Barack Obama

Juan Ortega

Network Marketing

Marriage

Married My Best Friend

Hopelessness

From My Writings

Foreward

Positive Thinking, Willpower, and Determination

Being Soldiers of God are we ready?

Changing the Focus of our Thoughts can

Fear and the Destructive Things It Can Do To Your

Fear and It's Destructive Effects Part 2

Standing Up for the Little Guy - Motivational

Gratitude for True Friends in a Time of Need!

Behind the Captive Bars of Religion -

I Can't Envision a Heavenly Father of Love that

Sticks and Stones. A Treatise on Bullying and

Going Deeper into the Word

Why is it hard to picture ourselves as children

Genie In a Bottle Christianity

Positivity 101: Overcoming lies about ourselves!

Grind Time - Motivational Monday Blog Post

The Power of Decrees and Affirmations

Decree's and Affirmations Whatever Friday Blog

As Wise as Serpents | Friday Fun Day!

A God Who Rejoices Over Us

Balance In Life

Live in the Moment

The Real Enemy is Within

Holiness and Mercy

Perceptions and Truth

Trials Are Good For Us

Amazing Ways to Overcome Our Defeatist Attitudes

Unforgiveness, Just Let It Go!

Bootstraps

Darkest Before the Dawn

Speaking of Spirituality

Speaking of Spirituality Part Two

What's Next?

Chapter Two

Endnotes

Chapter Three

The Stock I Come From

I was born in the city of Denver, Colorado in April of 1979. My mother is such a beautiful woman. I love this woman with all of my heart. She is a woman of reduced mental capacity. My father was Elder Howard Sanford Denton. This man also was of reduced mental capacity. But I count it an honor to come from this stock. Let me talk about my father first. My father was a man who never accepted his mental faculties the way they were.

His parents tried to restrict him and what he could do. He was told that he never could drive. He would not accept that and fought to learn how to drive. This man with only a grade school education and developmental disabilities refused to accept the fact that he could not drive. He learned how to drive and bought a Volkwagon Rabbit vehicle.

A man of limited understanding. This man of great determination became a minister in my uncle's denomination. I am so grateful for his example and it's from him and my mother that I come from. My mother is another look from the same perspective. My mother was also restricted from living a normal life. She was married off young after the affair with my father because the two families agreed to it.

She was never allowed to live life according to her own desires while my great aunt lived. You will learn more about her in the next chapter. But while my great aunt was alive my mother had no choices in anything in life. I think my aunt did this out of wanting to protect my mother but I see it from the outside looking in. She was taught early not to think for herself and she only has excelled and soared once my great aunt entered the spirit world.

My mother began her own journey into the freedom to do what she wanted after the dominating force in her life was removed. My mother has the greatest life in the world according to her. My mother is a servant of the highest. She reminds me of some of the biblical characters she is in the church all the time serving God day and night.

My mother may not be the best theologian but she can pray like no one's business. Allowing herself to get caught up in the worship of the highest God it's so precious. I love watching my mother as she lifts up God. She is human with faults like anyone but she has the purest soul I know. She is my rock and example. She is always in my corner. I love my mother so much because I have an opportunity to see her on a daily basis.

Both person's lives culminate into me. I am the unique soul because of them. I have my father's complexion and my desire to serve God is the same as his. I have my mother's laugh, her emotional states, her passion. Both of them together have come to make me who I am. I love the difference's both of them have offered to me.

So before I get into the lesson of this chapter which I will do for every chapter in this book. I want to illustrate that neither my mother or father raised me. My great aunt Eva, the strength of my maternal family raised me. This woman moved from Tennessee with my grandmother and grandfather and their nine kids to only have her sister (my grandmother) pass shortly after coming to Denver.

This woman raised nine children by herself. And as if that were not enough she took me and raised me from the hospital. My aunt was in her sixties when I was born already. I can't wait to elaborate on the lessons my aunt taught me in the next chapter. But I have to admit that even though she has faults she did the best she could with what she knew how.

I will also state that I am especially proud of the city I come from. Being a Denverite is a true honor. I am able to be proud of the five points neighborhood where I was raised. It was a shining jewel in African American culture. I am so honored to have been a resident early in my life. I moved to Montbello in middle school another neighborhood that I am especially proud to live in.

So without further adieu let me introduce the lesson section of this chapter. Each chapter will have a lesson at the end. I did not want to just write a book about my life and the experiences I've faced but I also wanted to give you lessons I've learned. So I hope that you enjoy the lesson I've prepared below! Once you master it I hope to see you in the next chapter of my life and the next chapter of this book! Thank you again for reading it!

The Lesson

Always fight for what you desire in life. There will be some folks who never believe in your vision or dream. If your vision does not scare you it's not big enough. Like my father's vision of driving. It's a vision that scared him and everyone around him. If he would have believed the naysayers he never would have made it. But because he did not believe the naysayers he fought his way to driving.

If you don't know your purpose in life it can be found out simply by seeking God's face.

Prayer and self-reflection on what your good at in life will help you know what you should do in life. But no matter what you decide never be afraid of how big the idea is. God does not give us small ideas. I am so grateful I come from both my mother and father, it has helped me learn so much and made me a greater person.

Chapter Four

The Principle of the Streetlight

My aunt was a great woman. She brought her family from Tennessee and poor and poverty there to Denver Colorado. Along with my grandmother and my grandfather who was an engineer in the Army Corps engineers. My aunt struggle in life my aunt never had it easy. She works she raised 9 children that belonged to her sister. And then as if that was enough or not enough to say she raised me. The doctors at the hospital convince my mother that it was better for her to have a late stage abortion than to carry me to term. But God's plans will never be frustrated God provides an auntie to save the day. And so I'm going to get into the second principal pretty early and it is the principle of the auntie.

The Principle of the Auntie: God will never ever let the enemy frustrate the plans he has for your life. He will always provide someone or something at the perfect moment to help you in your life and to help prosper you.

God provided Eva Mae trail in my life to save me from death. She could have let them kill me she had already raised 9 children. But she would not see my mother's seed die. I owe my life to her and being an author I dedicate this book to the three women who have influenced me the most of my life. They were my mother and my wife and my auntie. My auntie, she worked for railroad company she works for different companies in even as an old elderly person she takes me home from the hospital and raises me which was a full-time job. I was not the best child. I was so disrespectful I had no respect and I got into so much trouble. I've done everything under mount switch from steel to assault friends too every manner of thing that you could do wrong as a youth without going to jail. My aunt, she raised me and never had Richard but we always have what we need it. I never went without good school clothes while I think that they were dorky because they were not Jordan Brand they were JCPenney Brand.

I grew up in Montbello Colorado. I was born on the east side of Denver, however, we moved out to Montbello in the 6th grade. And I attended the notorious Martin Luther King middle school. You were on Nightline for being so bad when I was in attendance there. Why you've had a lot of fun things in it though I was made to be my aunt's snitch. So because of that I never enjoyed a close relationship with any of my aunts or uncles except for my uncle Walter and his wife Roslyn and uncle James and wife. The rest of my uncles with pick up my cousins who stayed with us and take them out for different social happenings and whatnot involve me. And that was because my aunt made me snitch on their recreational activities. I didn't understand that you were not supposed to be a snitch at the time, however, I understand that now. I was isolated a lot in my life because I was not cool I was short like Gary Coleman almost and I didn't dress well and I not have steel in my spine like I did now. I was raised by a woman so I was always in my feelings and sometimes I still find myself always in my feelings.

Men stay in your child's life you have invaluable lessons to teach your children. I wish that my aunt out my father to be in my life and to teach me how to be a man and not to be a crybaby like I always was. Don't call me no punk. I used to finish fights with people three and four times my size. I used to be alone and I used to be by myself all the time. And that hurt me a lot in life. I used to wonder why I wasn't my cousins. Even to this day I still compare myself to my cousins. I know my cousins love me to death! It's just circumstances beyond my control that separates us. Your gonna get a bonus principle in this chapter, never separate family members from each other the damage can never be repaired.

Lesson

My aunt had a rule about when I had to be inside of the house. I call this the Principle of the street light. When I was a kid I had to be in the house when the street lights came on. This lesson is about knowing your own limits. Lives need to be formed by rules. We first obey the laws of God and then the laws of the land.

After we obey those first two groups of laws we must follow laws we create for ourselves. Some call this values. The rule my aunt had was for my own protection. And I feel sometimes we dive headfirst into danger and end up in bad situations in life. Just because something is not illegal does not mean that it's not wrong.

I believe that this is Satan's way of trickery. When we think that the law should be the only thing we follow. Even Luciferians believe that you can do what thou wilt is the whole of the law. This is not the way of God. This world is so perverse nowadays and I believe it is because you have done away with your values. I hope that you enjoy this lesson this may be a hard one to swallow. I will always keep it real about my life in this book and always keep it real with my lessons. See you in the next chapter of my life and ready for a next lesson!

Chapter Five

The Bello's

I grew up in a neighborhood known as Montbello. I think I told you that. The bello's were a good neighborhood for the most part. Yes, we had many gangs in the area. Gentrification was at work in Denver at the time. We grew up on what is known as the East Side of Denver. And the East Side had those old nice brick houses. The East Side was known as a black ghetto neighborhood growing up. But the homes were phenomenal and the people watched out for each other. In the nineties, money started flowing into the East Side. And people started buying up the homes quick!

Some of my dearest friends in the church live on the East Side of Denver, Colorado. And if you told me as a kid that urban white professionals would live there I'd laugh you out my house. But that's why we moved to the bellos. The "man" came and offered Auntie a grip to move and so we did. Montbello was a crazy experience for me. It was the first place I had really tight friends. I would say that I lived in two cliques. One was a family that lived down the street from me that became a second family to me. And the other one was a bunch of friends from high school. The friends from high school kept me out of trouble big time!

The ones on my block were the ones I'd get into it with. Though one thing is for sure those ones from my block are the ones still around while my friends from school are still around but suspect because we're not really in each other's lives anymore. The friends from the block became family. As two of the sisters from that family married two of my cousins. I thought it was a match made in heaven. I thought it was dope. But I would go through a lot of stuff with my family. And a lot of experiences with my friends. I and my friends were the geek clique of the bellos. Ever since middle school we did things like Bible Club, Shakespeare Festivals, etc

    I was a smart kid but I was not motivated. And fighting to prove your no punk because your Gary Coleman size kinda prevented me from doing my best in school. In high school, I was unmotivated because of the fighting and my great aunt who raised me getting sick, etc. So my grades suffered except for my sophomore year when the Scott Family came to town. The Scotts were my cousins, my aunt Lucille married my uncle Scott. (that's his last name but that's what I and the rest of the fam call him). And when they moved in all the fights ceased. I had two big swole cousins who are my sworn protectors to this day watching my back. I love my cousin Fred. We go back like flats on a Cadillac. I have to tell you the tale.

As a three-year-old child, I still had not taken my first step. I refused to do so. I was a set in my ways kind of lad. And my whole family could not get me to walk. And if it was not for my favorite cousin in the world Fred I may not still walk. He came over to my playpen and took me by the hand, stood me up and started walking with me. Now mind you he's younger than I am! But he's always been a leader. That's my ride or die right there. He's been my favorite cousin from that moment.

Now back from the past, well that far in the past. When the Scott's came to town all the bullying of me ceased. The first day of a sophomore year of high school three football players came to punk me as usual. And as usual, I was prepared to go to work with my equalizer.

Lesson "Law of the Equalizer":

I was Gary Coleman short and I was faced to fight guys six feet and taller. My aunt taught me NEVER start a fight. But if one is started with me, finish it. So I would pick up anything I could that would help make the fight fairer. If they were six feet tall footballers, I was grabbing metal trash cans, whatever I needed to go to work. And that's what I did, I went to work sending the can crashing on their heads. Now as a latter-day saint I don't advocate any violence, but I make this a principle because in life we face some astronomical challenges. There are tools to help level the playing field. Never compromise your soul or your dignity to level the field. I do not condone cheating, etc. But use prayer, fasting, faith, hard work, extra study, etc to level the playing field. Get you an equalizer!

Now back to the story! As I was in that hallway about to go to work without escape I was so scared. But to glance a Warren G song "I glanced in the cut and I saw my cousin Nate.." He and Fred were right there and jumped on those football players. My Uncle was called up to the school because all three of us were getting suspended. And I remember my uncle Scott asking us what happened. We told him that I was about to be jumped when they intervened on my behalf. The principal expected yelling, punishment, etc but my uncle smiled and said: "That's what family supposed to do.."

I'm so grateful for my cousins. They been my ride or die forever. I don't know what I would do if I lost them. And last year when I was in the hospital fighting for my life from heart failure it was them who were right there. They had my back! They prayed for me. Now I did my best in the bello's but situations came to bear that forced me to drop out one month before high school graduation. That was the roughest experience of my life because it was also when I faced homelessness for the first time in my life.

My aunt was robbed by people she put in power to take care of her affairs. They sold her house from under her not even caring that I an eighteen-year-old had a place to stay. They sold all her insurance policies, burial plots, everything this seventy-year-old woman had amassed in her life and used it to buy new cars, a new house, and more for their own family. She was placed in a horrible nursing home and I had to move in with my aunt and uncle. My aunt and uncle were like parents to me anyway. They had come into my life around seventh grade because I knew the bible cold. I even knew eschatology subjects back then and could speak very eloquently on the bible.

They took me under their wing and I grew up in their church. At the age of fourteen, I taught my first Sunday School. At the age of Sixteen, I did my first mission with Child Evangelism Fellowship. At the age of Seventeen, I was ordained a Youth Pastor. I loved being Minister Green. But I was not ready for that life yet. I messed up telling a lie to my uncle and was demoted. But I didn't care. I wanted to be like my uncle when I grew up. He is still a role model of mine until this day. I love him so much! But I was not destined to be there long Heavenly Father had other plans for me.

As I look over my formative years in Montbello I think about all of the experiences I had. They actually naming the man that I am today and I'm so grateful for them. I have to shout out the Brooks Family which have become my family. I grew up living down the street from the Brooks family. The Brooks family married into my family via two cousins of mine who I talk about in this chapter. My experiences growing up I would not trade for the world.

As I write this we're getting the Easter time in the family likes to come together to celebrate. The Easter egg hunts and barbecues are usually all the rage. They taught me how to celebrate. I do remember some of the themed parties that we used to have. I remember the haunted houses that we used to make from scratch. That house was the most popular house in the neighborhood on Halloween. Everybody in the family portrayed different characters for the Haunted house. Then after all the trick-or-treaters were in bed we would have some of the best Halloween parties ever.

Even though my childhood was very rough I am very grateful to have grown up in this community. I think about the Boy Scouts of America in my time in that troop. Which is a perfect Segway into the next chapter talking about my friend Rick who is also a scout and his dad the scout leader? However, before we go into the next chapter I want to teach on a different principle.

Lesson - "The Law of Balance"

In our lives, it is so easy to bring things out of balance. Gluttony is a sin not because God does not want you to have things, but because he knows that too much of a thing throws things out of balance. It causes things to be out of whack. When I think of this I think the times in my life was out of whack. It usually is because I have done things to an excess. In life, there is what I call the law of opposites which I will talk about in a different chapter. The law of opposites simply stated is that there is an opposite for everything in the world. For good there is evil, for God, there's Satan, for a male there's female and more.

For our lives to be in perfect equilibrium we must practice balance. There is such thing as too much of something. Have you ever had a dessert treat that you love so much that you could eat all day? And if you ate that dessert all day? I bet you would get sick of it pretty quickly! Now, what happens if he eats it once every few months? It's almost as good as sex, well not quite but you get what I mean. How do we find balance in our everyday lives? Finding balance begins with introspection into ourselves. It culminates with the conscious planning of what we will do or not do, etc.

Chapter Six

My Best Friend Rick

I want to tell you about my best friend in the whole wide world his name is Rick. Me and Rick go back like two flats on the Cadillac. I met Rick in the six grade but I don't believe we became friends until the seventh. I thought that I was hot stuff, and I treated people that I thought were less than me really badly. I was a geek. These are things that I'm not ashamed now because geeks run the world. If I only had half the smarts as my friend Rick.

I could tell from very young that he was very gifted. I was a dumb geek if you could believe that. While I hung out with those that you would call geeks none of us really were except for Rick. We were the special ed crowd to be honest. I think Rick took pity out on us but don't tell him that. Rick was in advanced placement classes that's how smart this man was. I was more the politician of the group I wasn't very cool but I knew people and people knew me.

I remember walking to school everyday with Rick. And that was a long trek. We walked a mile to school every single day. I remember some of the conversations that we used to have on this walk. I'm going to give you a pro tip, "never abuse your best friends". I was horrible to Rick. There were times in school when people picked on me and I took it out on him. I used to pick fights with Rick, but he would never fight me back. I write this chapter on Martin Luther King Day he was my Martin. No matter who fought him he took it attitude of nonviolence.

I never understood until now why he always took this approach of nonviolence. It is because he took his religion seriously. I think I was a fake Christian in high school. Don't get me wrong there were times when Jesus was closer than a brother in high school. But I did not show the peace that this man shows. Even to this day he is a man of nonviolence. I never thought that things got accomplished his way. I now realize that his way, is Yeshua's way. True Christianity is in the actions not feeble prayers or church attendance. True Christianity is shown in those actions when no one is looking.

Rick might not have thought that anyone was watching but I was. Even as an adult when I chose a different faith he remained a friend. When I was sealed to my wife he was present as my best man even though he did not believe, nor does he believe in Mormon ordinances. He has shown the true love of Christ and is my greatest example of how to be a Christian. I'm just now learning lessons he had command of at age 13 - 14.

So to breakdown the lessons I learned from Rick.

Lessons Learned from Rick -

1. Never bully anyone you never know how much you're going to need that person. In times of my life where I've had the most trouble Rick has been the one constant friend. Has he been the perfect friend no, neither have I. There are times that I wish that Rick could've been there for me but I did not communicate my need.

2. Always communicate your needs. There are times in my life that I wish I had my road dog by me but I didn't tell him that he was needed. When I had heart failure he was not by my side because he didn't know. Rick's prayers can sustain me and I don't want him to get the big head when he reads this. But I don't call him super Christian for nothing.

3. Never take out your anger on anyone else. As a youth one thing I wish I could

correct was the starting fights with Rick for no reason. I was mad that someone had beat me up and instead of dealing with that anger I wanted to beat someone else up. And I knew Rick would not fight back. He was an easy target. But as I look back over my behavior which was reprehensible I want to cry there is so much about my childhood that I wish I could take back. That is one of them.

4. My last lesson for this chapter is simply this a true friend sticks closer than a brother. I feel honored that his family has adopted me in as one of their own. His mother and father have become my mother and father, his sisters are my sisters. That's what a best friend relationship looks like. Rick and his family love me no matter what. There are those in my own church who don't have that lesson down. I weep for people who don't have that

level of love because I feel that either they are babes in their walk in Christ are not Christian at all. In any case I am thankful to have Rick as my best friend and I pray blessings of God over his life.

Chapter Seven

Latter Day Saint

So now we're at the chapter about me becoming a Latter-Day Saint but that happen. Well, I'll tell you I live with my aunt and uncle who took care of me after my great-aunt was put into a nursing home I say put into a nursing home because she made someone else her power of attorney and those people took her money and put her in the shadiest nursing home ever. And I was on the streets and my aunt and uncle were kind enough to take me in and I love them to this day like parents because of it. But living in that home they didn't have any friends all I did was go to work and come home go to work and come home and go to church on the weekends and here and there we go out to eat or on vacations with my uncle. But they have their own marriage and so they spent a lot of time together then too and I spent a lot of time alone watching TV in my room and this was before they had children or foster children. And so one day at work I met these individuals they were missionaries of the Church of Jesus Christ of Latter-day Saints and they befriended me.

Our friendship started off with me arguing Doctrine. I had seen many movies like Temple of the god makers. In all these movies had told me that Mormons are evil that Mormons were wrong that they were the most horrible Church in the world that they really didn't follow Jesus Christ and I believe that I took it Hook Line & Sinker. But over time we continue arguing doctrine they gave me the Book of Mormon several times but I never read it I always threw it away. But one day my friend Eddie gave me the Book of Mormon and told me to read it and he told me that if I never found out that the Book of Mormon was true from that experience that he would never bother me about it again and I thought that that was a good deal. Song on the bus ride home and the bus takes about an hour to get from where I was working to home I read the book of Mormon I mean I scoured it and then I prayed on it I said Lord if this book is true to let me know somehow I snuck it into the house and I went to sleep that night I woke up at 3 o'clock a.m. with a hunger for the Book of Mormon like I've had for the Bible. And that was how I knew that the Book of Mormon was true I told Eddie the next day that the Book of Mormon was true and he suggested that I meet with him and talk with him about it that weekend. So we met that Saturday and they explained the plan of salvation to me and as I listen to this missionaries I knew that there were true.

They asked me to make the biggest decision of my life I was to become a member of the Church of Jesus Christ. I thought it was a member of the Church of Jesus Christ before. But I was only doing my best to follow Jesus with the knowledge I had at the time. I found out there was more to follow Jesus and as I knew that I knew I had to join. Elders Wolf and Beesley were the Zone Leaders at the time (leader missionary types) and they were the ones to interview me for worthiness to be baptized. I had to know the decision I was making. I did not know the sheer impact of would have upon my life. It would be the most important decision ever made.

After I was baptized I had to leave where I lived at. My uncle was just as we testament said if you can't control your own house how can you lead the church. And I had chosen to unite with a church different than his. I had chosen to become a latter day saint. I left his house two days after joining and embarked on a crazy adventure that I'm still on to this day. The Lord had always been faithful. He has always taken care of me. He promised to never leave me and while sometimes I feel like he has, he hasn't. And while he's never left me he did not promise things would be easy. To the contrary every since I decided to follow

Jesus my life has been a living hell! But he has helped me through it all. I testify that Jesus lives and is the savior of the world. And he is at the helm of the church I am a member of. I have a testimony of this!

Lesson: Dare To Stand Alone

Dare to stand alone. I think that this lesson goes hand in hand with the lesson from the first chapter. When I became a Latter Day Saint even though I had many friends and supporters I had to stand alone. I don't ever think I would be experiencing life on such a level if I did not have the audacity to stand alone.

I had a vision for my life. And I did not truly know it until I joined the Church of Jesus Christ of Latter-Day Saints. If I did not make a stand for my life I'm sorry to say that I would still be in my uncle's basement. I don't have my uncle I love and look up to him. But had I not undergone a faith shift I would not have lived on my own, I would not be married or experiencing the fullness of life that I am living right now. God came that we might have life and live it abundantly.

But its not always an easy journey to get to that abundant life. Sometimes you have to go through many trials and adversities. Sometimes you have to stand alone. Sometimes you have to shed tears. But to get to your goals you have to be willing to stand alone.

Lesson: Never Be Afraid to Fly

another crucial lesson that I learned by being a member of the church of Jesus Christ Latter Day Saints is never be afraid to fly. I think of my life pre Mormonism and I see I was very sheltered. I was like a chick that was in the nest who did not know how to fly. When I joined the church I had to live on my own. I do not know where my meal was coming from, or how to pay the rent. I knew nothing, but learned it all on the fly. I had to be pushed out of the nest essentially in order to discover that I have wings.

Is this something in your life that you've always wanted to do? Is there a goal that you always wanted to achieve? Is it big, I hope so because God's plans are not small. We dare to dream we began to move in the divine. Where we utilize our faith even if it's of a mustard seed we can move mountains. That is what the Bible as promised us in Matthew 17:20. So exercise your faith today! No dream is too small for God. Those that make it usually do so because of their great faith. Whether or not that faith in God or not, faith is a divine principle that is set forth in the universe today. You will see in later chapters why I believe in the secret that Rhonda Byrne has revealed in her book.

Had I continued to be afraid to fly I would not have the fullness of life that I have no. Part of this fullness of life comes from my beliefs and religion. But also the bulk of it comes from the experiences that I was able to have because I took the chance to play. It was stated that I was retarded and would never accomplish anything in life. They even stated that I would not even graduate high school, which I did ask the class valedictorian at Great basin high school in Clearfield Utah.

They tried to convince my mother to abort me because they believed I would not have a good quality of life. But look at me now you're reading my words! As you can see God can do anything if you have faith in him. In 1st Corinthians 1:27 it talks about the Foolish things to confound the wise. I am one of those foolish things of the world. The doctors said I would have a poor quality of life. I laugh and mock what they have said. Does my life have challenges and struggles? You bet! Probably more than the average man and woman in the world. But God has brought me through victoriously! God has done a miraculous work in me! He has helped me grow and he is helping me to not only live but THRIVE! I am so blessed and I can hardly contain the excitement I feel. But guess what? If I never had been forced to be on my own I never would have these experiences and I would not be where I am right now. So I encourage you to look to yourself and not be in the same situation as i. Don't wait on situations to force you to fly but take that leap of faith and fly today!

Chapter Eight

Seaman Green

I found myself in this new Faith being a Latter-Day Saint and it hurt me to the core because I lost my home. I lost everything that I had I had nothing. I was homeless I was on my own for the first time in my life. I had just lost my auntie to her having to go to the nursing home and it devastated me and so I I tried to find solace in my faith and I did and people in my faith were so loving and so awesome. I remember this family the Ransom family who took me me in like I was their son. They help me every step of the way. Every major ordinance of the Gospel they were there. Every shining achievement in the church they were there and sometimes not even knowing, I mean they just showed up for instance the day that I was at the temple receiving my Endowment. They showed up just to do a session they didn't even know I was going through for my own. I sat down and I looked over and I saw her I saw Sister Ransom and her daughter.

But back on point so after I had joined the church I was really kind of floating in existence. I didn't really know what to do my life. And so I entered Clearfield Job Corps. Clearfield was the obvious choice because it was in Utah. I really did not have that much of a choice I think I had the choice of three locations Montana, Western Colorado and Utah.

I didn't even want Montana because who want's to go to Montana? I know I'm probably going to have to do a Fireside one day there and people will probably be upset at me. You know what, it's rustic it's majestic, I get that. Montana you know it has its charms but for a city slicker like me that grew up on the Eastside in Denver that was not for me. And Western Colorado well while I like the mountains being Colorado and I did not think that I was really going out of my own living in western Colorado. So I entered Job Corps in Clearfield because it was Utah it was the Mecca of the Mormon faith. It is the headquarters of the church and so I entered there and I didn't really know what I was going to do with my life. I spent my time there just living. It helped me not to be homeless on the streets I really had no purpose; no plan in life.

I bounced between dozens of religions because for the first time I was on my own and I was being treated like a grown man and no one could tell me anything. Now I always attended the LDS church out there but I was a part of so many different religions it will make your head spin. It pretty much was about how I was feeling for the week. One week I was Pagan and I'll let a huge Wiccan circle out there. It was like 15 people and I was the high priest and I did not know what I was doing and I really thought I was serious about it. It looked cool and I saw the movie The Craft and I was like this is it! I'm going to do it and like I said I think I had that coven if you want to call it that for the space of about a Week. Or maybe it was a month or two. I remember that I hung out with a African Prince. I don't know if he was Nigerian or Liberian but he was a prince from Africa and he was rich and he was a close friend. And he was Muslim and he's like "hey you want to be my friend you have to convert to Islam." So I had my shahada in the mosque of Salt Lake City and I hung out with him. But I was never a serious Muslim now I probably would have been excommunicated from the church had they known that I was going to all of these different religious Services. I mean I think I did some of them just to get out of class early on a Friday afternoon. Islam was cool cuz I mean it's Friday I get to go to Jumah Service. And again It was in the afternoon on Friday so you got to get out of class early and I thought that was too cool for school and wonder how come the Latter Day Saint religion that has services on Friday.

I attended a Church of God in Christ in Ogden because it reminded me so much of the church I grew up in. And my uncle's church that I left and it felt like home but no matter what I always attended the Latter-Day Saint Church. I just think that I always knew that that was my home. That that was where I was going to be and like a like a swan Treading Water. I did so many different trades at Job Corps because I do not want to leave Job Corps. I wanted to stay there forever however that was not possible I took a tile setting, Auto Parts specialist for the United Auto Workers. I took culinary arts which is what I'm good at today. I burn (in a good way) in the kitchen! I'm a chef and I cook so official! If you don't know go check out my blog and see the recipe each week and I'm so official! Look at the resume and skills! I also did the Police Officer Training and retail sales manager course. I did the ROTC program because I just did not want to leave Job Corps I graduated Job Corps finally with my high school diploma and I was a Cadet major in the ROTC program and I did so many trades that job corps was like you have to go! Get out of here!

I was not ready to depart on a Mormon Mission yet and I had no clue what I was going to do because I cannot go home! I was going to be homeless if I really had no place to go so I joined the United States Navy. Now I didn't do what I wanted to do in the Navy which was the Cook or Chef, because that MOS military occupational specialty was not available. So I joined the Navy as a hospital corpsman and the Navy was good until I failed PT test. And when I failed this test I had to depart the Navy and they also found out that I had a slew of other health problems and so I had to return home. If there is one lesson I learned from my time in the Navy I will tell you this the one lesson that I learned in life never quit.

Lesson: "Never Quit"

In life sometimes things get too as things get us down and we don't know where we're going. We have nowhere to go but up and you just feel like nothing is ever going to work out for us. But the main thing I could stress is how about not quitting! As a matter of fact it's still lesson I still battle today so I there's anything I could teach you through this chapter my book is not to quit. Because you're gonna learn about me and my mission next and I am so ashamed because I really felt that I quit even now I don't feel I'm a RM even with an honorable release for health because I did not fight to go back out. Even though i was honorably released from my mission the because of Health issues and I feel if I fought harder I could have reached more people, so DON'T QUIT!

Lesson: Never Underestimate Yourself

Life is tough sometimes. And sadly enough we deal our worst blows to ourselves. I know I talked myself out of both my Navy and Mission experiences. Before I could even begin I already had defeated myself believing myself to be weak and inadequate. If I knew then what I know now I would be writing this book from a way different position. But I guess that's why it's a book and it was God's will that I do what I did. Sometimes we do not take into account our potential and not our current state. We look at where we are now and talk ourselves out of some of the best experiences of lives. I want you to stop where your reading and write down in the margins of this book or in a notepad your dreams. I don't care how small or how big they are. The bigger the better because your dreams should scare you! You will see in later chapters when I talk about leaping and flying that life is meant to be scary sometimes.

But if I can impress something upon you is to never give up and never underestimate yourself!

Chapter Nine

Elder Green

Kenneth Neal green you have been called to serve as a missionary of the Church of Jesus Christ of Latter-Day Saints you've been assigned to labor in the Georgia Macon mission when I think of the day that I receive my mission call I know that God Lives. There are so many ways that he showed me he lives he warned me I say where but I believe not one but had a revelation to me that I was going to be called to the South and I need to prepare myself. I really didn't understand what the whole prepare yourself yet I thought maybe he was talking about the physical rigors of the mission. Or maybe he was talking about the people that I would teach that maybe they would not receive the possible who knows what the Lord meant. But my mission was an experience I was not the best missionary of Jesus Christ. Combination I got into it almost physical altercation with my trainer I testify that Revelation is true and you need to let Revelation work when I went out on my mission my first companion and elder care I'm not going to give his name but he was the brother younger brother of my roommate from Denver Colorado so when I got there I asked the missionaries the 8-piece the people who help the president if I could be assigned with older kids. Me and older team oil and water it was horrendous I was not humble I was not ready as a 2425-year-old man had been in the Navy had experienced so much in life I was not ready to take orders from a 19-year-old punk. He wasn't a bomb at the time I probably would have had a few more Choice words to describe him besides the punk word but I was not ready to take orders I was not ready to humble I was not ready to listen and I only did I forced the hand of Revelation but my body gave out on me. The week that I entered the Missionary Training Center in Provo I found out that I was a diabetic I have been using the restroom 15 20 times a day now if your missionary that means that your companion has to go everywhere that you go and my companion was not happy with me I'll have any get up and use the bathroom, as a matter of fact, he had some Choice words for me before I ended up going to the medical center I can't go to the missionary clinic and they could not find out what was going on and so they sent me over to the BYU clinic and once I was at the BYU Clinic it was there that they did a blood test and they came in the room and they said older green we're sending you to the hospital immediately and I said what for why you sending me to the hospital and they said your blood sugar is 1013 we have to send you to the hospital.

Spent a week and a half in the hospital I was going to be a missionary I did not watch television, as a matter of fact, the nurses commended me on the fact that I was obedient and other missionaries that were in the hospital took the Leisure of breaking rules. I would not break rules and so I studied hard and even though most of my MTC experience was in the hospital I was able to go out on time with my missionary class to Georgia.

So we pick the story back up in Georgia and I pushed and feet I was assigned to Elder k and the younger brother or my roommate. And I thought because I and roommate got along so well and me and him we're going to get along like famously. I was wrong I was so wrong verbal altercations we almost we had a shoving match almost physical altercation it was so bad the Zone leader had to interfere. Now I had a bad attitude when I don't mention anything that you can learn from this chapter is don't quit and check your attitude at the door.

Because another day was a good missionary and you know a lot then I probably could learn a lot but our personalities just completed so hardcore. And that combined with health issues combined with the fact that I was serving in the most racist Mission ever. I am not going

.

to comment on some of the racism encountered by members. Because it's ugly and I just want to leave that part in the past because I did encounter racism from Latter-Day Saints. I never thought that I would and realize that I had met before then was super awesome and super positive. But there are people with ugly attitude and I'm not worried though. And so dealing with the health and health got worse because I got diabetes and it came with a vengeance and the long walks and we had to take because of being in the country and the diet that we were under my body just shut down I stayed out in the mission as long as I humanly could and we did some good out there I did read somewhere otherwise the person so we did good I wonder if things are going okay because when I came home for my medical I was released medically because diabetes just hit me so hard and I did not know how to handle the disease and I couldn't work and that made me have to go back to live with my aunt and uncle.

Something I never thought that I would do something that I did not want to do. My aunt and uncle are great I love them to death I still look at them as parent figures in my life. To this day I love them and they're a flawed way of trying to protect people from the world from the influences of the world and bad people and bad choices I had to live a very sheltered life I'm inactive for a period of about eight years while I lived with my aunt and uncle. I was not allowed to be allowed to say that I was not allowed to read the book of Mormon kind of threw myself into their church I became Anything Green because I don't want to make the best of the situation but I was trapped and it was going to be very negative time in my life it would be the only time I like that I attempted to commit suicide and I did it twice singing for my life where I had absolutely zero help I didn't have any friends I didn't go anywhere I stayed at their house wasn't really allowed to use technology or have a few days I would sneak out and meet the bishop once a month for lunch at a subway and just cry Bishop Frost and such an awesome man and I loved him so much. He kept my records active for eight years even though I was inactive. Me giving up on my mission put me in the darkest place of my life. So my lesson is trying to be humble! Be loving and never quit especially on yourself!

Lesson: When the Going Gets Tough, FIGHT!

It was not my place in life to fight my illness. A lot of times you can be caught up in the what should have happened. Heavenly Father had a plan for my life and I would not be here teaching you this lesson. However, I want you to avoid my pitfalls. So learn this. Had I not quit I don't know where my life would be. Don't make my same mistake. When the going gets tough you get tougher!

Chapter Ten

Disability

Living with my aunt and uncle made my health get worse. My diabetes through and so many complications of diabetes. My depression became very real and very dramatic and very great. And it was very scary to me. I was in such a dark place and I want to speak to people that have disabilities that God has not forgotten you. I thought I had forgotten me not that I was doomed to never have a life to never have a wife to never enjoy the things that I'm able to enjoy it today. I think God all the many glorious blessings that he has given me and my family. Because even though I had nothing if I had Jesus and that's all you Jesus will bring you through any situation when I lived with my Uncle I attempted suicide twice and now they probably read it. The people that lived there knew of my overdose on insulin. Attempt one I did 100 units of insulin and slept in a day, time two I did a hundred and fifty units and slept in two days and had to be wakened by their kids.

    Hopelessness is a horrible place to be in and that's where I was at the time. Depression is a disease it is a physical reaction. And it has shown itself in many ways. I remember thinking that God had made me for nothing. I love my uncle and I still do to this day. They did nothing but try to give me a roof over my head and clothes on my back and they did the best they could they didn't know I was doing with the pressure they didn't know about me my health issues really. So as I lived there as time went on I didn't move into a phase of hopelessness and that's what I'm going to be talking about in my next chapter. So if you learn anything from this chapter no this hold on help is coming. Trouble don't last always God has not forgotten you. If he said he will do it it will come to pass and I love that lyric from this Deitrick Haddon song that says God has not forgotten. God will never forget you. He always has you on his mind. So don't quite don't let go keep holding on trust in Jesus Christ our savior loves you he understands your pain for you slept through it all and he will bless you

People deal with disabilities each day. Because of my father and mother had a variety of disabilities I inherited all of them. These did not develop late in life but was there from the very beginning of life. I dealt with Learning Disabilities early. Thankfully not on the same degree that my mother and father had to deal with it. My endocrine system did not work from birth. Essentially meaning every hormone your body makes mines did not. I had to do hormone replacement therapy since I was born.

    My endocrine system has led to diabetes occurring in me. The Diabetes I think of as a gateway drug. It makes everything else worse. With diabetes quickly came neuropathy and retinopathy. Soon following came cataracts, then following that came heart disease. Along with the heart disease came heart failure which is what caused me to die three times.

I have fought and survived three bouts of cancer. My life has had a lot of downs. But I believe that I was allowed to have these things because in my weakness I find strength in God. In my life, I have been able to glorify God through my weakness which brings us to another lesson.

Lesson: "Dependency On God Is Not Weakness"

Because I am so weak in my body I have had to learn to depend on God for everything. God always has made a way in my life. I am so grateful to God and many people will be turned off by these statements. I'm surprised though because I've been religious this whole book.

I like the idea that a man is at his strongest point when he is on his knees in prayer. Dependency upon God is not a weakness but a strength. I am so grateful for this lesson in my life. I know that God lives and I know that he looks out for us. God gave you that big dream. God gave you that scary vision. God will make a way for you.

Now dependency upon God does not mean he is going to do everything for you. You would be wrong and very mistaken. God will make a way but you still must accomplish it. God will show you what to do but you must help yourself. I'm tired of these faith-based preachers who promise riches and dreams through false prophecy causing people to become imbecilic and not working towards your own goals.

Abraham had to step out on faith and do the action for God to look out for him when he left Ur. Moses had to physically return to Egypt to be God's mouthpiece to demand the freedom of the Jewish nation. Jesus Christ had to choose to be obedient to his father in all things for his work to be completed upon the earth. Each of these men depended upon God and God blessed them. But it still took action. Read your word people! Read your word and don't stone me for knocking your favorite televangelist. There are many evangelicals preaching sound doctrine. But if you believe that because you send some preacher your money that God is going to give you pie in the sky I got some beach property in Wyoming to sell you. Send me your money instead. I hope you can get the candor and humor in my above statement.

Forgive me for being a little too raw in the last paragraph. But I will get off my soapbox now.

Chapter Eleven

I Need A Angel

I want to talk about love and compassion. As I think over my life I'm so blessed and highly favored of the Lord. I don't say that because the Lord swooped down and did something for me personally though he does do that. He likes to use other people bless me. I've had these people influencing my life ever since I was born. I like to call these people angels. We can all be someone's Angel. The first angel that comes to mind dates back way to my youth. Her name is Colleen.

Colleen Bryant I think is her last name was someone that my aunt brought into my life at a young age. I don't know how my aunt met Colleen but it was a kingdom connection for sure. Ms. Bryant as I like to call her as a kid used to come and pick me up and take me over to her house. Sometimes she would pick me up and take me to the museum or the zoo or some other cool learning attraction. The trips were always fun but they always were about learning. I don't think that we did a trip that was not about learning. Every Christmas and for my birthday Colleen would give me a present. These presents were always involve learning. She made learning fun, but she also showed me how people with wealth live.

The next angel or I should say angels that I want to write about are the people I call my church parents. I was 18 years old when I joined the Mormon church. And immediately after joining the Mormon church I had to leave where I was living. So not only was I embracing a new religion in a new way of life. I was having to live life on my own for the very first time. There were two people at my baptism into the Mormon church. They are the Ransoms. This family adopted me. They made sure that I had a place to live with another brother in the ward. And they help me understand this Mormon religion that I knew nothing about.

These people loved me. And I did not deserve it. Every major moment as a Mormon these people were there. My church father stood at my confirmation, ordination to the priesthood, and call on a mission. The church mother was there for all those events. Her and my sister even surprised me at my endowment. This is a funny story that you should read. I went to the temple to be endowed in preparation for serving a full-time mission to Macon Georgia.

I remember that I arrived at the temple with my bishop. Having grown up a Christian these rituals and ordinances were very strange to me. Let's keep it real I still don't understand fully. After having gone through the beginning stages of the ordinance I look over and see my church mom and sister. I did not tell them that I was going through the temple that day. As a matter of fact, they lived in a whole different city but somehow the Lord guided them to do a session, my session. Even my Doc Martens that I wore on my mission were purchased by them.

Even since the mission, they had been involved in my life. It was because of them that I got to see Yellowstone for the first time. I got to see Idaho Falls. There were so many times that they just took me to dinner, or talk to me when things were going bad. I never met more generous people in my life.

The last Angel that I want to talk about is my friend Sanddy Javins. Our friendship is not perfect. I think there was a lot of us taking advantage of each other. I would always call her when I needed help. Or if I needed a ride to the hospital, or needed something from the store, and even rides to the airport. And if you don't know the airport is super far from me. She would take advantage of me because of my technical genius. I could be called to fix computers, printers, phones, and even television sets. But one thing I have to say about her is that when I need her 99.5% of the time she is there.

What I want to teach in this chapter quite simply is anyone could be an angel. There are tons of more angels that affected my life. But I don't have time to write about the mall. I would even say that my wife is the best Angel of all. We all have people that have been sent to minister to us. But we must also remember that there are people we've been sent to minister to.

Chapter Twelve

How to Overcome

I want to talk about overcoming. So many people deal with adversity in life, and they let it defeat them. I know I let it defeat me many times. I deal with adversity just getting up in the morning. Every morning that I'm alive is a miracle. I have a list of affirmations that will leave you awe. I have diabetes, I have every complication from diabetes. I have congestive heart failure, coronary artery disease. I suffer from kidney failure. And to top it off my endocrine system does not work or function.

I could easily let it defeat me. For a lot of my life, I did let it defeat me. A lot of my life I let it get to me. Because of all these physical issues I've suffered from emotional and mental issues. Chronic depression is something that I've dealt with all my life. So on top of physical infirmities you have mental ones. How do you overcome when you have so much stacked against you. It's quite simple first you have to become determined. You have to become determined that you deserve the best in life. On my blog, I often talk about believing the lies the enemy of our souls tells us tells us.

We are the sons and daughters of deity. We are joint heirs with Christ Jesus. Do you understand what that means? The things that he did we could do. We have infinite possibilities! Even as I write these words I'm in pain. My foot has a really bad ulcer. But I don't claim sickness. I serve the living God who is able to heal and mend. I'm able to write even though I'm dealing with physical affliction. Meditation and prayer is key to my success. Through meditation and prayer, I can connect with the God of the universe. I can make my request known to him, my Abba father.

I don't think that people really understand who they are. You're special to God. You don't have to be super spiritual or one of the spiritual giants do have access to your father in heaven. You don't have to be a prophet or an apostle, or biblical figure to have intimacy with God. Once you understand that and you enter into an intimate relationship with God you can understand who you are. Then the trials and afflictions of life begin to seem small. And as they began to seem small you began to see your possibilities. And as you see your possibilities, you begin to believe in yourself.

Chapter Keys

1. Believe in God. Your victory in life begins when you establish a relationship with the one who made you. I can't stress this more than enough. Not until you get to know him, will you ever understand who you truly are.

2. Commune with God through prayer and meditation. This is how you will get to know him. And as you get to know him, you will get to know yourself. He will reveal to you what you're made to do. He is the potter and we are

the clay. This step takes a bit of submission. But as you submit to the God of heaven and let him mold you, you will begin to have victory.

3. Believe in yourself! As you get to know who you are you will begin to see that you are a son or daughter of God. Let that sink in a second. You are the child of deity. I'm not one of those new agers who say that you are God. Because no one on this earth has arrived there yet. But I will say this, as a child of God you can exhibit your father's traits. Believe in yourself! Trust that you got this!

Chapter Thirteen

Emotional Control

Growing and evolving is hard work. Today a neighbor assaulted my wife at work. I thank God that I'm on a whole new path. You may call it cowardice but I call it an improvement. Back in the day, I would make mistakes that could get me in jail. I've made a lot of mistakes in my life. I think at times I've been very dishonest and conniving. There are times where I let my temper get the best of me. I want to share a few instances where bad decisions have cost me greatly. I do this in the hope that you will not make the same mistakes.

The first time that I can think of well not the first time but the first instance I will tell you about is in high school. The nation of Islam had held a special assembly at our school. The local minister of the nation at that time was Jamal X. He came with the speech on black pride that stirred something within me. My friend Rick was the only white boy to be in the assembly. I must say I respect Rick because not only did he have the stones to go. But he stood up to the minister and questioned him on his racist beliefs.

I was not strong as my friend Rick. I wanted to belong, I wanted to be part of something. So I started spouting racial epitaphs that Jamaal X had used. I started saying things that were characteristic of black Muslims even though my best friend was white. I am so ashamed of my behavior that day. Now that I look back over my life I've delved into one thing after the next. In job corps, I explored all sorts religions. Everything from Wicca to Islam. I did not make the best decisions in life. And certainly, I was an unstable man.

    You see I hope that you can learn from my mistakes. They have taught me many things, and have prepared me for what I'm doing now in life. I believe I am well-rounded because I had these experiences. But you can focus on God without making the mistakes I made. Elohim is God. Yeshua is the son, the Savior of the world. I went through almost all the religions in the world until I found a relationship with the maker of the world. And when I had established this relationship I knew I was home.

So often in life, we let our emotions trap us into making bad decisions. When I acted like I was Nation of Islam that day I hurt my friend. I said things I really did not mean. But it was emotions that trapped me that day. Emotions are a barometer of our life with God. The enemy of our souls likes to play with our emotions. He likes to trap us without logical thinking. You can know where you're at with God by your emotional state. The enemy comes to steal kill and destroy. So when we have negative emotions we know that the enemy is at work in our lives. But when we have positive emotions most likely God is at work in our lives.

How do we know if God is at work or the devil? Because sometimes the devil comes as the angel of light. Meaning, he is very deceitful. Sometimes when we feel good it is because of deception by the enemy. The enemy brings false happiness and joy. And his does not last. But the joy of God lasts forever. So, I talked enough about this subject whose ready for another story?

Without incriminating anyone, I remember back in the day a family member being assaulted. This was before my membership in the church of Jesus Christ of Latter-Day Saints. I was drunk this day. And when my family members were wanting to ride I wanted to ride to. I so wanted to be a tough guy but I was not built for it. My cousins I think always knew I had a higher purpose. That's why I was watched over like a hawk. They knew I was not built for it. There's no shame in knowing your moral compass or physical ability.

But my temper would not let me be dissuaded. So we rolled out and when we got there I was ordered to stay in the car. I respected the people doing the ordering and did not have the heart to stand up to them so I stayed in the car. That night they got in trouble with the law. And I escaped because I stayed in the car. This is one reason why I do not like alcohol or drugs because it alters who you are when you're under the influence. I've said the most reckless things drunk in my life.

Being under the influence of alcohol that night along with tempers flaring could've cost me a lot. To this day I do not have a criminal record. I can apply for jobs that require clean records. I avoided becoming a felon that night not because of good judgment on my part but because I wasn't built for it. And my family knew I wasn't built for it.

Chapter Keys

1. Control over your emotions is one of the most divine qualities that humans can develop. When you learn to control how you feel and don't let your emotions be your guide you become more like God. Emotions are a good barometer for your walk with God. But please be careful because the devil and his minions know how to fake emotions. They know how to invoke fake emotions in us, but the so-called happiness they provide is ever fleeting.

2. Check your emotions with your heart. Double check those with logic. The Scriptures say try the spirit to see if it's from God. If it is from God then it will hold up to those checks. If it is from God it will testify of Christ. But never go off half-cocked. Always perform checks with your heart, mind, and spirit.

3. Retain control of your mind at all times. In my religion, the word of wisdom is there for a reason. But even if you're not a Latter Day Saint this principle holds true to you. Have you ever seen how someone stone drunk acts? Then why would you allow yourself to be on that level of manipulation by spirits or drugs? This is crucial to self-mastery.

4.

Chapter Fourteen

The Book on the Exes

SIKE!

So, you want the juice? And no not talking about Orenthal. I'm talking about the gossip. Well too bad because this book has higher standards than that. However, I will share lessons that I learned from exes which may in some way out them and I'm sorry if it does. So here we go!

Jamila - this relationship went off and on for about four years. This is the chick that even though she was my girlfriend, she was more like a side chick. This girl was hiding our relationship from her parents. She would only come over in the middle of the day when her parents were away at work. The lesson that I want to teach for my relationship with Jamila is to never settle when it comes to anything life. I was lonely, and so I settled for a relationship that was fake because all he did was sit at my house and do nothing. I settled because I do not believe I could get anyone better. This chick was fine, but her attitude and mental outlook were all jacked up. I got mad love for her and I don't want to talk to him about her. Her life is her journey, and she must come to realizations that she is not an adult yet on her own.

Sarah - Sarah is a very sweet girl. She is still my homegirl to this day. We all talk on the phone anymore because I have respect for my wife and I don't believe that men should be talking to any of the axes on the phone. But we do communicate via Facebook and social media all under my wife's watch eyes. This girl had my heart for the taking. I wanted to make her Mrs. Green. But like Jamila, she has her own family problems that prevent her from a marital relationship now. Like with Jamila I believe I was in his long-term relationship because I settled. However, that is not the lesson that I want to teach this girl. The lesson that I want to teach him this girl is simply communication. When you're involved with anyone in a relationship communication is king. If you are not communicating the relationship is dying. Don't be afraid to speak up and say what you feel!

Shannon – Shannon was my very first girlfriend in life. She was the sister of my homeboy. This girl taught me about treating people right. I want to tell you a story from my youth. I was 13 years old or so and off to a Christian camp on the other side of the state. This camp was awesome and I sat next to my homeboy's sister on the way up to the camp. I believe I asked her out in the van and she accepted. I spent the first couple of days by her side always until a girl came to camp that everybody wanted. However, this chick seemed to be flirting with me and spending lots of time with me. So, what do I do, I ditched Shannon for this other chick. I'm so ashamed and I want to take a moment to say I'm sorry to Shannon publicly. On the way back home I was suffering from an ear infection. This trip was over eight hours long. I started in the lap of the cute girl singing R Kelly's Bump and Grind. But soon as we came down the mountain I began to hurl violently. I threw up all over the cute girl and she did not want anything to do with me. I found myself out of her lap and at the front of the van. And who do I see? You guessed it, Shannon! This girl even though I had dogged her out took care of me. She nursed me and showed me true charity. Besides my wife, I don't think I learned more from anyone then I did her. It's weird because she was in the same apartment complex as I do but she is a great friend of mine and I value her!

Chris – You want to do the dirty. Here you go! I identify as a bisexual or at least bi-curious. I only have feelings for my wife. However, it is not to say that I have not explored the same-sex. I did have a romantic relationship with a guy named Chris. I don't have to be excommunicated for my church because they did not have sexual relations. But I'm not afraid to be a little transparent here and thank him for the lessons that he taught me. He taught me how to be as gentle as a dove. You would think I would learn that lesson from a woman, but his mind was as gentle as it up and I will always be appreciative for the lesson he taught me.

I find it important that as I tell autobiography and self-help book about my life that I include things about my previous relationships. I want to be as transparent as possible and have my readers know all my struggles set up under. This chapter has given you a glimpse inside of my mind in helping about relationships. Being bi-curious has been really tough for me. However, I know for a fact that I only loved one person that is my wife. So, I would not be doing this book any justice if I did not talk about her in this chapter. Because while I can evaluate in the get my exes in my past situations she is my future, she is the present, she is my everything! The mistakes I have learned from lessons listed above and the people listed above are all in preparation for my eternal relationship with the one I call my wife. I salute her and all she does for me. There's only one person on the throne of my heart and that's Jesus, but standing right next to him is the queen of my life, my beloved wife.

Chapter Fifteen

Barack Obama

I titled this chapter, Barack Obama, not because I love this president. I don't hate him either. But I do sympathize with him. I was elected as Resident Council President of the Tower at Speer in 2009.

I talked a little bit about me getting a place. But let me illustrate more about where I live. I live in a place that is specifically for disabled and senior adults. This place has many people who don't understand many things in life.

I felt called by God to help this place. And so I worked with another resident to found the resident council. We lived in a place that was horrible. There were open door drug sales, prostitution you name it. This place was in a huge mess. So working with other residents we founded the Resident Council.

This would begin a time of service that would last approximately nine years. It took much out of me doing this but I was not able to work and this was my outlet to get out of the house and help people. I would be called upon at all times of the day and night.

I even had to use it to do things for people I did not want to do. I officiated in three funerals here at the building. It is a tradition that when someone dies from this building that they hold a memorial service here at the building. People knew I was a Mormon "Elder" even being a service missionary at the time but they did not know that Elder's did not do funerals. I obliged because I loved the people who had died.

So your probably wondering why this is a chapter in my story. I think before last year that this was my legacy to the world. Is this place getting worse off than it was in the past? Yes, it's slipping again because I did not have the stamina to do this job for a tenth year. But it is a lot better than it could be. I am so eternally grateful for the work I was able to do because I know for sure that I had an impact on this place where I live.

Even to this day I still deejay at building events and parties as service to the community. I love music so very much. It has been something that has consoled me and healed me. Sharing this passion with my friends brings me so much joy. We dance the night away at these parties. But back to what I wanted to bring out in this chapter.

The Lesson: Never be too big to serve.

Sometimes our lives are in holding patterns. I believe that we need to take time to serve others. Your vision from God should do two things essentially. The first thing your vision should do is glorify God. God wants the world to know of his love. He want's the world reconciled back to himself. And he does this by blessing his sons and daughters who obey him. The first key part of the vision you're given by him is what can it do for him. Don't think this is selfish of him because whatever his vision is for us will prosper us and fulfill us. But it should also glorify him.

The second part of what your vision should be is that it should serve others. When you're serving your fellow brothers and sisters on earth you are in the service of your God. Never be afraid to serve others. Never be afraid to do things for others.

Sometimes it is hard to do. Sometimes people treat us foul. Sometimes there is deep-seated hurt in our hearts because of things that people have done to us. But I promise you that as you do you will grow closer to God. God serves us all the time right? And we are learning, in essence, to be a close to God as we can. So we must serve others and we will develop those divine attributes that make God who he is.

I am excited for what the future may hold. As we get near the end of my book we shift to talk about how we can be more fulfilled in life. I am so blessed at this point on my life. I feel I am finally living the life Christ promised in John 10:10

Chapter Sixteen

Juan Ortega

Juan Ortega...

What local mind would not be complete without talking about my favorite hobby? So, you probably wonder who Juan Ortega is. Allow me to introduce you to the Cubano maniac. Juan Ortega was my very first character in a LARP called the mind's eye society. Back then it was called the Camarilla. I joined this club back in 2006 after I became independent on my own. I was in a new apartment and I had no friends. I heard about this club from playing an email game called Jyhad Nights. This game was created by people who worked at White Wolf publishing the company that produces the vampire the masquerade series.

Being a man was hard for me because I was used to people always taking care of me. I had lived with my aunt and uncle for many years. Before that I had lived with my great aunt Eva. So, this club became my social outlet because I had very few friends in the church. This club has been my escape throughout life when things have gotten tough. I'm able to create a character in for a few hours escape my reality and be that character.

LARP is also the way that I have been able to stay sane through all my troubles. The friendships that I built have meant the world to me. I know that these friends truly care about me. I've had many of my first experiences in the club. My first experience with alcohol, my first experience with the opposite sex. Some would say that those things are bad in trying to judge the club based on those experiences I've had. However, those experiences were my choices and they have helped shape why am today.

This club has allowed me to travel to so many places. I love going to conventions and people knowing just why am, or having heard about my characters. I can't say that I know the whole club, but I can say that I'm known by many members of the club. I remember my very first to mention that I went to it was in Aurora Colorado, no scratch that is in either Milwaukee or Detroit I forget which of the two conventions came first in my club buddies can probably educate me better on this. I remember hanging with my friend Jae and playing vampire till early in the morning. I remember going to after's at IHOP and other restaurants talking about game and other social things.

This club has helped make me a man because it has presented me with opportunities both good and bad. I had the opportunity to do many things that are rejected because I'm a son of heavenly father. I believe that we must have diversity in all situations are also will never prove ourselves worthy of the divine birthright which I will talk about later chapter. This club has given me an opportunity to serve others.

We raise money for charity, give blood to blood banks, and much more. This organization even has a scholarship fund that uses to help its members to go and get an education. I am so proud to be a member of the mind's eye society. Asus a that with a bit of a reservation in the past because of the Christian connotations that are held against LARPING and games that we play. Many would accuse our games of being devilish or evil. However, I do not find this to be devilish or evil at all.

I know people a variety of faiths were members of this organization. I know Latter Day Saints for members of this organization. I know people of Christian denominations pastors even who are members of this organization. So, I want to shine a light on this. You can choose to play an evil character if you choose. And I think all of us been guilty of that in the club at one time or another. I would rather play an evil than to be evil and act out people in real life. I think that LARP gives you an opportunity to explore that in a safe confine. However, most people that I know usually play characters that are good or have some good to them.

Not a bunch emo kids that believe we are real vampires or warlocks. We are doctors, lawyers, pastors, and politicians play this game. We come from all walks of life. We come from all different religions as well! We're not Satanists contrary to popular belief. I never have and never will worship Satan. I never have nor never will portray character that worships Satan. So, I want to talk about some of the great stories I could portray.

Chapter Seventeen

Network Marketing

I call this chapter reach for your dreams because I had a dream once. I dreamed that I was a very successful network marketer. I had an experience where I bounced around from company to company and never really made the money I I thought I deserve. The type of money that I thought I deserved was being a millionaire. But I was not putting him in the network and when you're not putting in any work effort and you're not going to get anything. Because it was a saying in life, you don't get something for anything. I personally joined prepaid legal in 2009 and I was introduced by my friend Mike Black who was trying to make director at the time. Now to make Director you had to have a certain number of managers in your organization. I went from associate to manager within three days which is fast for that company. I think that the initial success that I experienced and the payday that I experienced set me back greatly because I expected it to come that easy.

    When the success slowed down and I did not realize my dreams as fast as I thought I would I became discouraged. I began to do what a lot of people Network Marketing do which is a jump from company to company. I think I fell in love with the idea of being in business for myself but not actually being in business for myself. It's easy to say that you're a network marketer or that you're running your own business. But when you're not making a dime when you're not really accomplishing anything. So, if you're involved in network marketing I first think that you need to evaluate if you really have what it takes to run your own business. Not everyone is made to be a business mogul or CEO. So, I want to teach the first lesson I've learned through my time in Network Marketing which is the Lesson of Seed Time and Harvest.

Lesson: Seed Time and Harvest - in this chapter I want to talk about paying your dues. In light must all pay our dues, I liken it to planting seed and harvesting. Planting seed takes a lot of works. You must kill the ground, dig holes, and plant the seed. It does not in their because you must fertilize the ground, water the seed, and ensure that it receives plenty of light and sunshine. Whenever you have a dream you must apply this principle to the dream. Take for instance my dream of becoming a well-known author, I'm not sure how many people will even read this book. But I do know that the book won't write itself. If I do not write the book then it will never come to pass. Whether I sell one copy, or thousands it will never come to pass and I don't pick up the pen and start writing, or tap the keys in my case. We can't expect life to magically appear for us we must want it. And when we want it we must have the determination and the drive to go get it. I am so lucky and blessed to have realized this. Over the past few days after I found out that my original publisher was closing their doors I have had a sudden burst of activity and passion for bringing this to pass. I think that the bad things that happen in our lives can sometimes motivate us and drive us towards good things. A lot of people would look at their publisher closing their doors as a bad situation. I see it as potential because I'm no longer writing my book for another, but I am writing it for myself because I read the benefits and rewards of all the proceeds. But at the end of the day that also puts the work on my own shoulders. I am responsible for bringing this dream to pass.

Being a network marketing cast also challenge my integrity. There were tons of times when I was not the most honest person in my business dealings. There were times where I tried to get over on the company's that I was hired by, or customers that I sold products to. I did not see my integrity as being important but the result of being more important. That brings me to the second lesson of this chapter.

Lesson: The Only Two Things I got in this world are my Word and my Balls!

Some of you have never seen the movie Scarface so he will not get a reference that I use in the lesson. But that is a direct quote from Tony Montana was portrayed by Al Pacino. If I can be a little transparent here, I must be honest and say that I've not been the most honest person in life. I think that if there is one saying that I personally wrestle with all the time is honesty. I was taught from a very young age to be fearful. I will be so afraid of getting in trouble that I will lie. Lying became a habit that was very difficult to shake. I can be honest in saying that the sin of lying will be one I wrestle with until the day I die. It is so important to be a man of your word. In Revelation, it promises that liars be cast into the lake of fire. Think about that for a moment? Lying can send you to a place of torment.

There's one last lesson that I want to reiterate so I will call it a mini-lesson in this chapter because I've already discussed in other chapters.

Mini Lesson- Don't give up! Don't ever give up! I think of where I can be if I would've to work prepaid legal to the best of my abilities and not quit I can be a millionaire right now. There are many things that I have missed out on because I've given up. So, if you can learn anything from me, learn never to give up! Again, I say don't give up!

Chapter Eighteen

Marriage

Aging out into a family Ward was very tough and it is a tough thing to deal with. To all my people approaching the age of 31, I empathize with you especially if you don't live in Utah. Because In Utah they have middle singles wards so the single activities and things get to continue.

However, when you're in a family ward those things do not continue. I had very few friends and I was very from the first time

I joined the family ward. The first Sunday I sat next to a girl I thought it was. Her name is Sammie we are still close friends to this day.

The first couple years in the family Ward the courtship continued even though she moved away to Mississippi I still kept in contact via Facebook and sent her letters and gifts. And then I flew down there to see her and meet her mom and her sisters and grandmother work down there and it was great we and we look into each other's eyes deeply.

And I thought this is wifey this is the one that I'm going to marry and so by the end of that trip I proposed and she said yes. Her family was moving back to Denver anyway and her mother had an apartment so the way she moved in with me with each other even though it was a month before our sealing date and I stay in the living room she stayed in the bedroom we kept it pure.

And things were going great until about a week before the wedding. All of my friends and I mean all of them about 15 people backed out of the wedding they said that they would not be there for me they would not be my best men my groomsmen bridesmaids a lot of people backed out and they said Kenny was afraid that you're going to make a mistake.

So I got on my knees and I ask my heavenly father, I said Lord if marrying this girl is a mistake let me know now so that we don't get sealed and find out that we're not compatible and cause all sorts of problems and so when I prayed that prayer I woke up the next morning and she was having some issues and the Lord showed me clearly that she was not the one she was not ready for marriage

I was not ready to do with marriage it was a very nasty breakup involved church leaders and officials I went inactive for. It was nasty. Sometimes we have to really pray and be careful what you pray for because sometimes the world will give us the answer and it might not be the answer that we want I don't want to marry that girl so I can fit me into the family Ward and I wanted to be able to have a wife with me at church on Sundays in thought that she was it. I was blind I was not paying attention to the signs and we didn't talk for many years because of that.

I'll continue living my life as a Latter-Day Saint but I became a Jack Mormon I've had no friends and family Ward cause we're going to take a second and give a message to everyone if you're in a family ward and especially your middle singles or anything people in the war that don't have friends befriend them I would have avoided Temptation and repentance and having to speak to the bishop if I have friends in the local Ward that would call me and hang out with me and would be there for me.

So I didn't have it so I'm going to Jack Mormon I drink I just I did everything underneath the sun I'm thankful I didn't go too far that would make me get excommunicated from the church but I was like I was a live wire. 2 years meeting Rachel she was a friend of mine from the building and she was. But when I saw her enter the Waters of baptism in the back of my head I said I bet she's my wife. I didn't think about it we went on for the next two years as just Friends. I was always the person that she called for blessings when she was sick There are some

Dangerous times in her life and she just needed back up. I saw her date many people and I always disapproved because I saw how they treat her and I'm so sad that they made her cry.

Especially one individual that called himself her fiance and I just thought in the back of my head that this Choice daughter of God does not deserve to be treated this way. I never thought to ask her out on a date because I was 14 years her senior still in 14 years her senior. And I just thought that she would want to date somebody way younger than me. And so I didn't ask and then seven months ago 6 months and a week I think I'll go she told me that she had a crush on me. Now those are sweet words to hear especially when you single and you never dated anybody in the church except for my ex who we almost got married. And this awesome girl tells you that she's crushing on you so I said hey we need today. That date or I should say not dating. I lasted 6 days before we were married at the city hall. She had a situation that was either going to cause her to leave the city or I marry her and I just knew that this was the person I want to be with forever and then take long we were best friends for 2 years and we knew each other when you were closed so it didn't take me long to decide that she was the one I knew in my heart and when she confirmed it that she knew that I was the one as well it was natural you got married. Part of me wishes that we would have more time to do it right which is being sealed in the house oh Lord but we have in 6 months we are going to be having our ceiling and we going to turn up for our ceiling we're going to be sealed and I can't wait. Someone said women are the bringers of joy and pain. I love that! Because marriage has given me so much joy and so much pain! But good pain, the pain of dying to self and becoming selfless.

Last year I died three times from heart failure. I always wondered why God brought me back. I like to think it was because God was going to give me the greatest gift of all, my wife. I like to think it was because I had more growing to do on earth.

Lesson: Love your soul-mates!

Treat your wives with all the dignity you can. God loves his daughters and they are worthy of our respect. Remember the angry daddy with the shotgun? Well God is like that father except he doesn't need a shotgun! Marriage is so sacred because through it you learn how the Savior loves us!

Chapter Nineteen

Married My Best Friend

I married my best friend!

In this chapter of my book, I want to talk about marriage. Marriage is the greatest state of the union on this planet. I married literally my best friend. She lifts me up when I'm down, she makes me smile we just a goofy phrase. I love her personality and everything about her. I want to talk about ways to make your marriage better than it is already even though I have been married that long myself so please indulge me. I and my wife's courtship was all of four days. When I met Rachel she takes my breath away. However, she is very young, way younger than I am. It is because of her youth that I never approached her. However, God had a plan and I do not know it. When I met Rachel she had just moved to Denver and she was very young. If there's one thing that annoys me is the fact that she is so young and sometimes refuses to listen to this old man. Now I'm not that old I'm all of 37 years old as I write this speeding towards 38. But I have lived life, and I've made many mistakes and I don't want her to make the same mistakes.

As we were friends I saw her in various relationships. Men treated her so awful that it really rubs me the wrong way. I knew if I had a chance I can show her real love and honor her as a daughter of God. She had to do some growing up first. I watched from afar as she matured and became a strong woman. She had a bastard of a father. I don't want to insult the man but he tried to sexually assault her and I got to be a safe haven for her. So when she told me that she had been crushing on me for the past two years I knew that my dreams are coming sure! We started dating immediately after she told me that and four days later we were husband and wife. We did not ask for advice from anyone, nor did we have a big ceremony. I made it up to her one year later when we were sealed in the Denver Temple on our year anniversary. Then we partied like rock stars!

I knew before we even started dating that she was the one for me. She drives me wild and I love every second of it. Our relationship has had its trials and tests, but we keep Christ at the center of our relationship and it is because of this that I think our relationship is so strong. The most precious moments in my life are times when I get to pray for my wife. I don't know why but there's just something about that! So enough of me rambling on and on about how I met my wife and I we got married let's talk about what I learned through marriage.

The first thing that I think I must sincerely highlight is marriage won't work if the couple is not selfless. In order for a marriage to work, there must be the compromise in all things. I usually control the TV remote at my house. But I've learned that sometimes I have to watch things that my wife likes. I might not be exactly the biggest fan, but I watch them because I love my wife. Now I know that's a funny way to describe selflessness and marriage but it is an easy example. I love to use those funny types of anecdotes, The next thing I want to say is communication is king. So many of our arguments have happened because of improper communication. We could have saved ourselves some trouble if we just spoke out loud. Don't bottle things up, I'm talking to you fellas! As men, it's super easy to bottle things up out of being "macho". Not wanting to appear weak and when we do these things we hurt ourselves so greatly.

    Ladies and Gentlemen: I entreat you to not keep secrets from your significant other. The relationship is doomed to fail when you do not share things and be open with your wife/husband. I know that one of our biggest fights happened because of a harmless secret that was kept over a valentines day gift and money. Which I won't go into because it's not for me to share me and my wife's business with the world. But this is a very big key I learned early in my marriage. Secrets just don't work so don't start!

Single men and women if I can give you a small bit of advice. Marry your best friend. Now I'm not saying for everyone to literally marry your best friend but what I am saying is that it's good to marry someone you have a strong foundation of friendship with first. Far too often we marry people out of lust or selfish reasons and wonder why our marriages don't work. So marry your best friend, trust me your marriage will be so much sweeter!

The last tip that I want to give is for the fellas. I got this tip from a very funny movie called Guess Who. This movie stars

Bernie Mac and was a white boy who was engaged to a black girl and all the problems that a father could cause because of it. At the end of the movie, Bernie Mac says to Ashton Kutcher the "white boy" that if he loved Teresa his fiancée then she was always right. He even asks Bernie "always?" And Bernie replies that she is always right. Fella's we had to eat that thing called pride. When it rears its ugly head it's easy to try to be bold and take a stand but in knowing so we always will lose because pride has no place when it comes to fares with a heart. She is always right!

Chapter Twenty

Hopelessness

Alright, my friend, we're getting into the good stuff we're going to talk about God and we're going to talk about how he helped me overcome. I was in a place of hopelessness never mind I'll go and I lived there for 8 years. There was no hope for me and one of my friends my good friend George lang shout out to you all this place where I could put in an application for housing. This place is a place where my father lived and their members of my church that I also live here. When I say the members of my church I mean at that time which was my uncle's Church. And so I put my name on the list and I forgot about it I continue living my life continue trying to pray and trying to read my Bible and trying to be a good Christian.

And about a year after I put in my name I got a call on my cell phone and it was the tower at Speer and that was the apartment complex that apply to and then told me your name is up on our list you need to come in and fill out some papers so I went in to fill out the papers. And I was told that the apartment is ready and you need to have your money in 3 days and if you have the money in 3 days were going to give the apartment to somebody else. I was not ready to move I have no money I felt in the biggest place of hopelessness that I tried to walk in front of a light rail train.

That's the last suicide atrempt that I made.

    I felt so bad that my friend George had to call the police on me. I was that suicidal. Talk about a place of hopelesness. I called the bishop and told him what was happening and he said don't panic, tell them you will have the money tomorrow. The next day came and just like they said they were waiting for me at the building with the check. God changed my circumstance from light to day over night!

    I had a new place and I never had a place of my own before. That day I went home and I packed all my things that I could all my clothes this Angela and my TV and my Xbox up. And the next morning as my aunt and uncle left for work I placed a call to a good brother in the church his name was Doug Perry and he came in his truck and we got my clothes and my TV and my Xbox and we left. I did not want to take the bed or the cabinets and dressers because I felt that my uncle and get those things. Even though I look back on it now I remember that I paid for them but oh well. I have my own place and they were not easy I was lonely I slept on the floor and then I have furniture for over a week I got my first couch off of Craigslist and thought he was giving it away for free

    I had to start from the bottom and it was tough all it was tough but I have the Gospel of Jesus Christ. I was able to return to church and I began to develop friends and I began to live a life of my own. I have a lot more to learn and hopelessness soon returned. I don't believe that it is something that we can always get rid of I think that from time to time it comes back. I began to look at my age and look at the fact that I was so low income housing low-income and I didn't have any money and I didn't have a career and I thought that no girl ever would want me. I aged out of the singles ward and I was brought into a war called the Capitol Hill work. And that word is now the city park which is the world I'm still at and this is 10 years later after living on my own for almost 10 years and not quite 2 years and I have a career as a Wi-Fi with family I want you to know that no matter how the situation looks we don't see how God sees so just focus on doing what God asked you to do walk hand in his hand walk step by step line upon line precept upon precept and you will get it you will get their.

Lesson: Hope Is a Reason for Being

\#

Chapter Twenty-One

Foreward

Before you dive into this section I would like to introduce it. Words in this section are from writings I have done on my blog www.simplykenneth.faith and I decided to place them here in this book because they have taught me a lot in my own life. I hope you enjoy this section of my best writings!

Chapter Twenty-Two

Positive Thinking, Willpower, and Determination

Positive Thinking, Willpower, and Determination Helps One to Attain Goals

Can you attain your goals with Willpower alone?

Willpower is, indeed, a great force in the world. The tenacity of purpose is in most cases a guarantee of ultimate success. On the contrary, a man who wavers at the first sign of difficulty, feels his confidence running out at the initial setbacks and loses enthusiasm at the first sign of failure can never achieve his goal. He is utterly lacking in the essential condition of success – willpower. Some tasks are seemingly impossible but can be accomplished with determination and hard work. One should not, therefore, lose courage in the face of difficulties.

Willpower can bring lasting results!

The efficacy of willpower can be demonstrated by numerous examples from the lives of common people. A person of the weak constitution who is constantly plagued with one or other ailment can bring about the vast improvement in the health merely by a pertinacious observance of certain rules. It may not bear instant results, but will certainly bring about dynamic change in the level of fitness.

Self-Examination is the Beginning of Willpower!

Similarly, a student can win distinction in the examination, if he sets his heart on it and applies himself with sincere determination. The reason why so many students fail in their examinations is not that the students lack the will to pass. They are indifferent to their failure or success, as they have no definite purpose in life.

Make Up Your Mind!

No impediments can stand in the way of a person who makes up his mind to attain his objective. There is a countless number of examples of people, who in spite of being physically handicapped, have achieved targets, which would appear impossible even to normal people. Such people do not allow themselves to be overwhelmed by the heaviest odds. Instead, they work systemically to minimize natural deficiencies to achieve their goals. They simply dare to defy their destiny by their hope, courage, enterprise, and dedication.

Positivity is Important!

Any man who pursues his ideals with determination is likely to meet with success. There are countless pupils, whose lives are a classic instance of the triumph of will. They have also known despair, failure, and defeat, but what puts them apart from others is that they do not succumb to these setbacks. They continue to work for the achievement of their goals.

You can do it!

A man with an iron willpower and a positive approach to life can certainly pave a way for himself in spite of obstacles and hardships confronting him at every step. The secret of success in life is to carry on steadfastly with eyes fixed on the goals! Everyone has within himself the capacity to work hard! We have the tendency to cultivate a strong willpower and optimistic approach, an invaluable asset to succeed in life.

Chapter Twenty-Three

Being Soldiers of God are we ready?

Being Soldiers of God are we ready?

Hardship is a way God trains his Soldiers~

My life has been hard this year. Even though I've gone through so much in life I think I am closer to God because of it. I want to talk about the nature of our relationship with God. It is not easy to take things in stride. I am probably like many of you who have gotten angry at God from time to time.

We as Humans or Soldiers of God should not get angry at our commander!

It's not the first time that someone on the path of discipleship has ever gotten mad at their master. In Numbers `6:15 we read,

"And Moses was very wroth, and said unto the LORD, Respect not thou their offering: I have not taken one ass from them, neither have I hurt one of them."

Moses was a prophet of the highest God and even he got angry and wroth with God and his people. So we as disciples of Christ are sometimes tempted to get mad at our creator. Maybe we don't like a commandment issued by God. Sometimes we like to think that we know what's better for us than a God in the far off yonder.

God knows a thing from Beginning till the End

As humans, we are guilty of making this mistake. And the sooner we come to a realization that he knows what's best for us because he sees a thing from the beginning to an end, and we barely see what's in front of our face.

Isaiah 55:8 - <u>"For my thoughts are not your thoughts, neither are your ways my ways, saith the LORD."</u>

His ways are not our ways!

We can remind ourselves that the Lord's ways and thoughts are higher than our ways. It's highly ironic that we dare get mad at the man who created the universe. God is not OBLIGATED to do anything with us except when we follow his commandments. He is not a man that he should lie.

Enduring Life Like a good Soldier

We have to learn how to be patient in this life. God has taught us in his word that even the bad things work out for our good. When we endure the tough things in life we build strength and endurance. This strength can be of great use to us in our callings and vocations for God. God is not wanting weak soldiers in his army.

Lessons from Boot Camp in my own life!

When I think about the boot camp I endured as a United States Sailor I think of the first day. We were stripped out of our "street" clothes and put into purple jogging suits we called smurf suits that had the Navy Logo on it. Boot Camp was about breaking down the years of bad training from our earlier lives.

Then we began to be built up as sailors and shipmates. When we join the Army of the Lord we have to be trained in how to live for

God. We spent most of our lives living for the other team, the devil. Our discipleship starts with changing the attitudes and ways we once lived. This is a sifting process. When you sift flour you are removing the unpure parts before baking.

God has a purpose for Adversity

I figure that is one of the purposes of the adversity that we go through in life. God is using it as a sifting process. It's easy to say that we Love God, but will we prove ourselves true when things are not right or when things go wrong in life. And before you say that is not biblical look at the disciples.

Sometimes as disciples of Christ we have to endure.

Disciples of Christ faced problems at every turn in the early days of the church and even when the master walked the earth.

Shipwrecked multiple times, thrown in prison, each of the first apostles save one died a violent death. They had to prove their loyalty to the master in ways most American Christians simply don't understand.

I look at the Christians around the globe who have their lives put on the line just for knowing the savior. Look at saints in China who are jailed for meeting together. Look at the Yezidi's and Christians in Iraq who have died at the hands of Daesh (ISIS) because they would not renounce Christ and become Muslim.

We are blessed to live in America!

We in America have it lucky. So when I think of things in that way I am grateful that the lessons I learn are easier. But be aware we are in the last days and there will come a day when American Christians have to pay for their beliefs from a regime that will be against faith in Christ. Soldier are you ready?

Chapter Twenty-Four

Changing the Focus of our Thoughts can Changing the Focus of our Thoughts can Revolutionize Our Lives

By Kenneth Green

How Changing Focus has Blessed Me!

It is interesting to me when I take time to figure out what I'm thinking about in life. When I reflect on the way that my mind can be distracted, it amazes me when people have a complete mastery of their minds. I respect the Buddhist monks who can meditate in a zen-like state. I am new to this meditation thing trying to incorporate it into my morning routine. And sitting there even doing a guided meditation with my VR goggles on I still find my mind wandering.

This has caused me to ask myself how much time do I spend wasted on thoughts that do nothing for me. When I reflect on the stupid things that catch my attention like Facebook or games, etc. I see a ton of time wasted. I'm not against those types of activities but what I want to advocate is a proper use of our age when we are to be productive. You can spend much of your time on the frivolous things and miss a lot of your life. I know that many Christians don't talk about meditation because they feel that is something that belongs to eastern religions.

Practicing Meditation

Christianity has practiced meditation in the ancient church. I don't know where the modern church got the notion that we should not meditate. Personally, I find it to be a great resource for me. Mindfulness and being present has helped me shape my perception and think in better ways. I am so grateful for this, but I'm off on a tangent time to reel it back in. So what do you think about on a daily basis? Some people think the "Secret" is new age philosophy. But it's even there in the bible.

What we say and think matters!

Proverbs 18:21 - "Death and life are in the power of the tongue: and they that love it shall eat the fruit thereof."

What you talk about or more whatever it is that consumes your thoughts are the power of life and death. By changing your focus, you can begin to live in an abundance of life that God has designed for us all. So how do we do this? I think the first trick is to make positive thinking a habit. They say that you can learn any skill if you put 10,000 hours into it. That's a lot of hours. I like what is also said that if you do the same thing over and over for nineteen days, it becomes a habit. That seems much more obtainable.

Starting a Daily Routine of Changing Focus

So here's what I'm doing and I think it can help you. Start each day with a morning routine. Do this for nineteen days straight to develop the habit and discipline it takes to do it. The method I'm using is from The Latter Day Morning which is a good book. But feel free to come up with your own! It starts off with me thanking God and being grateful for what I have at that moment. The more grateful a person is, the more open to more blessings that person is.

The next part of my morning routine is to do meditation. There's that ugly word again I know. But when I start with meditation it seems that I am more at peace. After that, I commit to writing at least 1000 words a day of content. Whether that's a chapter for my book or my blogs. And lastly, I journal. Just a few lines about the day before. I hope that as you practice this over nineteen days, you will be able to get your morning started off right and changing your focus will make you more productive.

Chapter Twenty-Five

Fear and the Destructive Things It Can Do To Your

Fear and the Destructive Things It Can Do To Your Body Pt.1

Everyone deals with fear...

What is fear? The Dictionary defines fear as "an <u>unpleasant emotion caused by the belief that someone or something is dangerous, likely to cause pain</u>, or a threat:" Fear is something that we each have to face in our lives. Oh how perfect life and the world would be if we did not have to face fear, but this is an emotion that happens to us all.

The Goal of this Blog Series

I want to illustrate in this blog series the damaging effects that Fear can ravage on our bodies. The problem with fear as shown by the statistics below is that many of us fear things that will never happen. So why are we experiencing this negative emotion that is not based on reality but on a possibility of what "could" happen?

Percent of things feared that will never take place 60 %

Percent of things feared that happened in the past and can't be changed 30 %

Percent of things feared that are considered to be insignificant issues 90 %

Percent of things feared in relation to health that will not happen 88 %

Number of Americans who have a diagnosed phobia 6.3 Million

Why is fear bad for us?

So now that we have begun to illustrate what fear is, now let's get to the heart of the matter and talk about why it's not good to experience this. I believe that this is one emotion that God does not want us to have. Think about it, are we trusting God if were fearing something?

My goal in writing this series is first to illustrate why it is bad to play into your fears. Then in my next post in this series, I will demonstrate some techniques to help overcome your fears. Fear causes a plethora of health issues. There are some health issues I've discovered in my research for this article that I did not even know plagued us.

Fear affects a molecular level!

First fear causes our DNA to become unbundled. I did not even know that fear affected us on a DNA level. When our DNA becomes unbundled, several dangerous things can happen. It makes it harder for our bodies to produce proteins, new cells, chemicals, and hormones. I had no clue that it even affected us on this level.

Fear Causes Men's Hearts to Fail Them

I believe that fear has a big part to play in some people having heart attacks and strokes. Anxiety which is a natural by-product of fear has a laundry list of adverse health effects, some of them are as follows.

Ten Effects of Anxiety or Fear

1. Raised Blood Pressure
2. Difficulty Swallowing
3. Dry Mouth
4. Dizziness

5. Fatigue

6. Head Aches

7. Irritability

8. Inability to Concentrate

9. Nausea

10. Rapid Breathing and More!

Fear has a laundry list of sorts when it comes to bad things that it can cause in the body. The list from anxiety above is rather small as the list does continue more and more.

Can someone escape fear completely?

Some Buddhist monks will probably disagree with me, but I don't believe we can. I think that as we learn more to trust in God and less of a worry that we can live fear free lives. However, I do not believe that one can completely get rid of fear. So how can we begin to live without fear? That's a real question. It's one that I want to delve deeper into in my next blog post, but there is one suggestion I'll get started with.

Trust In God Can Alleviate Fear

I believe that Love casteth out all fear. (1 John 4:18). As I thought about the verse, I just referenced I wanted to go deeper in my study of that verse. I believe that perfect love casteth out all fear because perfect love is GOD! God casteth out the fear. When we know that we have no one to fear but God (having Godly Fear IS a GOOD THING), I think that we can live lives devoid of fear, anxiety, and worry. When we trust in God, we know he has our best interests at heart ALWAYS and no matter how a situation looks like we know that God is still on the throne, and he still reigns with providence in our lives. I want to leave you with another scripture that seems to help me make it through.

Some Scriptures for the Road!

<u>2nd Timothy 1:7 "For God hath not given us the spirit of fear, but of power, and of love, and of a sound mind."</u>

May we trust in the God of the universe who has nothing but a good future in mind for us, In Jeremiah, it states that

<u>Jeremiah 29:11 - "For I know the thoughts that I think toward you, saith the LORD, thoughts of peace, and not of evil, to give you an expected end."</u>

Know that no matter how the situation looks now, God has a future for you. God has thoughts of Peace and not of evil towards you. Oh, how he loves us! I'm so grateful for his love that he showers us with. If we trust in him, we can trust in that future; we can believe that he is the captain of our souls and knows what he is doing! I can't wait to see you in my next blog post, and I hope this has given you some useful information!

Chapter Twenty-Six

Fear and It's Destructive Effects Part 2

Fear and It's Destructive Effects Part 2

Never Let Fear Conquer You

Let's talk about the destructive effects of fear in this part two article! This week has been pretty rough on my family and me. I found out that I was being extended a "release" from a position of responsibility in the church. This is a natural thing, in our church, you usually don't have people who serve as leaders for decades on end. Unless you are in one of the most crucial roles of the church. Even our Bishops are extended releases after a period. And when I heard this news fear gripped me. Fearful that I was being released for wrongdoings of a few months back it had an adverse effect on me for sure.

Learn From What I Say, Don't Do what I do!

This is something you hear a lot growing up in the African American home. But I say this to you with all of the love that I have within me. As a human I let that fear conquer me today. Instead of being productive I stayed sleep for most of the day depressed and wallowing in that fear. I wasted a whole day! I'm glad I did not stay lying down, but I could have.

How can we overcome our fears?

When I started this series, I did not want to focus on my fears. But when I began to think about how we deal with fears I had to evaluate my concerns themselves. So I've illustrated in my last post the adverse effects that fear has on us. Now I want to talk about how we can overcome them. Because what good is it to focus on the negative things? So I think the first thing that we have to look at is what causes our fears? I believe in God, and I think a lot of it stems from a lack of faith in God. If we have faith in God, we can trust that what happens to us is going on for us.

Overcoming Fear Helps Us to Become Strong. The Stronger we come, the more easily courage comes.

Courage is a rehearsed emotion. Many of the trials that come in our lives are to help us learn lessons from them. As we overcome individual trials and hurdles, we increase in our belief that we can overcome anything. And if you trust in God as I do, you know that as long as you have God with you, you can overcome anything. So the first part of overcoming fear to me is knowing you are human and that fear is a reasonable reaction to certain issues sometimes. When you're able to sense yourself becoming afraid you can begin to be analytical of your feelings and your ability to start to be courageous which is the opposite of fear.

Step One in Overcoming Destructive Fear is Knowing When you have fear!

Step one is knowing that you're afraid. I know that sounds very simple, but it's more complicated than you can believe. Today in Sunday School I taught on honesty and mostly what was said was that being honest with ourselves is probably one of the hardest things to do. We like to lie to ourselves because we don't want to believe in bad things about ourselves. But in my last lesson I talked about the by-products of fear, use that as a list to tell when fear is around.

Step Two in Overcoming Destructive Fear - Recognize That Fear Is Rooted Deep in Us!

A different website talked about that fear can be rooted in traumatic events and childhood. I agree with this assessment because a lot of times we don't have current stimuli for fear but are regressing through events of the past. I'm also one to think therapy with a therapist can do amazing wonders in this regard. I can be sincere in stating that I have a therapist! Part of me is so sincerely grateful for her help in my emotional well-being.

I am also taking classes in Christian Counseling because I want to start a practice coaching and helping others! But we need to recognize whether we are fearful because of our immediate surroundings (i.e. being afraid in a tornado or a robbery situation) versus past events that can be triggered by current events which are unrelated (i.e. rape in the past cause you to have a fear of being around men, etc.i)

Step Three In HowIDeal With Fear is Trust in God.

This is where I verge off the common path that most therapists or blogs have. I believe that when we come to God and we grow in our relationship with him our fears all go away. I believe in what the Bible says on the subject.

"There is no fear in love; but perfect love casteth out fear: because of fear hath torment. He that feareth is not made perfect in love." - 1 John 4:18

It is stated in the bible that God is Love. If he is in love, then we believe in him we know that all things work for our good (Romans 8:28). When we have faith in him we know that every event in our life is orchestrated by him and if we trust and have faith in him we know that these things too shall pass. This year has been very tough for me, all of you who have read my blog know this. But I have learned so much about God and his love for us this year that while I wish I did not have to pass through this, I've learned that I've grown through this.

In the next part of our series, we will continue to delve into ways we can overcome fear in our lives! I hope you have a blessed week!

Chapter Twenty-Seven

Standing Up for the Little Guy - Motivational

Standing Up for the Little Guy - Motivational Monday Series

A Tale from my past! I Was the Little Guy!

Never be afraid to stand up for the little guy! I remember when I was younger and I was of very short stature. Life was very tough for me because I did not have the finest clothes. My great aunt did the best that she could but being Gary Coleman short with big attitude caused loads of fights. I remember my junior year of school and the first day the football players were coming to punk me. My big cousin's Fred and Nathan were there, and I distinctly thought of the Warren G song Regulators when they commenced to beating the football players. Then all three of us wound up in the office, and my uncle Scott was summoned. We were so scared that we would be in trouble, but he was proud of us because we all stood together. I think it's memories like that in me that has birthed the activist.

What kind of motivation Monday topic is this?

What a weird topic for Motivation Monday I know. But I want to motivate you to stand up for the little guy as well. So many times in life people are made little by more than just stature. In my apartment complex, we have a lot of people who are not as mentally acute as they should be. There are people here who have an ignorance of the law. They don't know their rights they have as protected citizens. I hate when people assume that folks should know things because of their age.

I'm the Activist for the Little Guy today!

In my apartment complex, we have someone here that is abusing other residents. This has caused the rebel in me to rise. I hate when someone picks on developmentally disabled or emotionally troubled people. This person not only messed with those types of people but specifically he messed with my mom and wife. Now the ghetto in me wants to stomp this dude out. But the Christian in me wants to handle this via the rules and regulations of the hud housing.

Standing up for people 101

So how do you stand up for the weak? You have to know what they want. Speaking to people, you can begin to understand how to fight for people. We can make the same mistakes that the aggressors make by fighting for the weak without understanding what they need. Have you considered that they may not want you fighting for them? We must be careful that we do not make the same mistakes that other people make when it comes to standing up for the little guy. I know if someone just jumped into one of my fights as a high schooler I may have ended up clocking them just for not minding their business. But when my cousins did it they asked me what happened and how we wanted to handle it. See the difference?

Combat the self-centeredness attitude!

Greediness and self-centeredness is a plague amongst our generation. There are so many things out there that say "Mind your Business..." or the classic "Stop Snitching.."

I laugh when I think of these things. Satan want's us isolated because we become easier targets that way. When we look at me me, we miss the whole purpose of life. So the first thing I want you to understand in standing up for the little guy is that it puts you directly in the line of fire. You can get hurt doing this. But then I think of what Jesus would do, and he put it on the line for others often.

Don't alway's expect thanks or gratitude!

The second thing I want you to understand is that it's a thankless job. If someone has stood up for you in the past let them know how much it meant to you. But when you go into standing up for the little guy sometimes they don't appreciate you. If I could think of my eight years of service as Resident Council President here at the Tower I can count on both hands the thank you's I get. I even DJ'd the parties that we would have, and I would get more complaints than thanks. So don't get into this for the accolades you will be let down for sure!

In Conclusion

In conclusion, I want to challenge you to look for the little guy in the world around you. There are so many opportunities to help others and make people's lives productive. Approach them and be genuine with them. Allow them to communicate to you. One of the biggest problems that the "little guy" faces is the simple fact that no one listens to them. Don't make that mistake; please don't! Last but not least know your strength. You are not Superman. If you are not a tenth dan in Tae Kwon Do, don't act like it. If you are not a legal expert, don't offer legal advice. Knowing your strengths is half of the battle. And believe me, you may think that you are not talented, but each person has talents that God has given them that can be used for others.

Ideas for Causes to think about!

Some Causes that I would love to highlight for you are as follows.

- Causes involving Immigrants (both Legal and Illegal) they are often targets of victimization. What happened to this being the land of the free?

- Causes involving orphans. Being an orphan SUCKS! I know because while I have my mom, she does not know how to be my mom. When I lost my great aunt, I became alone in this world. There are times I wish folks stood up for me.

- Causes involving developmentally disabled adults.

Chapter Twenty-Eight

Gratitude for True Friends in a Time of Need!

Gratitude for True Friends in a Time of Need!

Trials keep coming!

I'm grateful for friends in our times of need! Yesterday was a very trying day for my wife and me. A dog bit my wife, and it looked pretty dangerous. I love marriage but hate those moments when you hear that someone you love has been hurt. I was upstairs in my apartment, and my mind was on preparing dinner. When I got the worst phone call, a husband could ever get. Your wife on the other line crying stating a pit bull dog just attacked her.

I'm not here to breed bad feelings for pit bulls. I think they can be an excellent breed; I believe that far too many owners own them for the wrong reasons. They own them for bravado, or they own them because they are fighting dogs. When a dog is trained to combat it does what it's trained to do especially if it's naturally aggressive.

Running For My Wife

I am sitting on two bad feet still that don't balance right and don't have proper strength. But when I got that call I found myself running down to the elevator and downstairs. I had 911 emergency on the one hand and calling friends in church on the contrary. I arrived downstairs and saw a very bloody Rachel. Sadness gripped me as I thought of what she was going through. I felt a range of emotions all at once. Sadness, Anger, a desire for revenge, and much more.

Awesome Friends

So my home teacher got ahold of me super quick when he found out what was going on. A brother in my ward, Joseph Glass was a superman dynamo. He called people like crazy and even biked over himself to the hospital. When I think of Christ-like service I think of him and my home teacher. Surprisingly enough my home teachers wife is my wife's visiting teacher, so they both came.

We had a great time cracking jokes and laughing with Rachel. We were able to be with her through it all. And the spirit was dominant in the room as we gave her a priesthood blessing. It was solemn, it was deep, and it was full of the spirit.

Christ-Like Love

This experience makes me think who I can be of service to today? Who can I help? Is there someone who needs my charity? God is amazing, and I love God so very much. I wish folks in the church would get this right. And I'm not talking about my religion per-say but the church as a whole, anyone who identifies themselves as a Christian. We love to wear the title sure, but do we honor it? Do we serve others with compassion, without expectancy of reward? My home teacher isn't even named in this article because I know I would rob him of his blessings by doing so.

Who Can you love today?

A relationship with Heavenly Father and Jesus Christ is not a one time get dunked and get the holy ghost and you were done. It is a relationship, and it's predicated on modeling them. As you begin to do the things that the Savior does, you will find others in need and help them. I like what he says in Matthew 25:35

"For I was an hungred, and ye gave me meat: I was thirsty, and ye gave me drink: I was a stranger, and ye took me in" - Matthew 25:35 (KJV)

True discipleship is not reflected by how many souls you bring into the kingdom. It's not predicated on a significant number of things you're known for. If God is love and was trying to be more like him, then that means we must become love as well.

Who is in need today?

I challenge you to look at the world around you. There are so many negative things happening in our world. So many people are hurting and in need of help. Sitting here waiting for my doctor appointment I wonder how I can help others. I look at so many people who may need a friendly word. Someone who may need a smile. Your actions don't have to be loud and pronounced. They can be simple and not receiving glory.

In Conclusion

I am grateful yes thankful for the trials of the past year. Trust me I know making that statement may challenge Satan to try us harder. Hopefully not as I could use a break, but one thing I know is that no matter what we face or come against as long as we have Christ he will meet our needs. God has stated in Philippians 4

<u>19 But my God shall supply all your need according to His riches in glory by Christ Jesus.</u>

Having Christ means that I will be victorious. Why will I be victorious? Because the praise and glory will go to him. And when he is victorious and gets the glory he makes sure that we are taken care of. Even though in

Corinthians 2 we if we are like Paul are likened to slaves in Christ's triumphant procession. But the Lord is so sweet and tender to us as he calls us his friends. Oh, how I love the Lord! Even though we are nothing and could be counted as slaves, he counts us as friends! God bless you and keep you my friends is my prayer! If I can be of service to you please let me know!

Chapter Twenty-Nine

Behind the Captive Bars of Religion -

Behind the Captive Bars of Religion - Motivational Monday Series

What is this series about Kenny?

As you have seen on this blog lately, I have been struggling with the testimony of my faith. I am so tired of being a wishy-washy flip-flopper of a man. One thing, Religion have caused my mental anguish of late. Life has been a struggle to me.

Was Religion meant to be a captive place?

I don't believe that Jesus Christ intended his faith to be a confined area. No, I think that Christianity was designed to bring liberty! James 2:12 states "So speak and so act as those who are to be judged under the law of liberty. " (James 2:12 ESV) We are now under a law of freedom. When I went to a prayer meeting of some Pentecostal's here last week they wanted me to renounce everything under the sun. Mormonism (that I understand as they are anti-Mormon), but things like how my wife and I have relations, or the love of travel, the kundalini spirit (which I never heard of) and much more.

This Christian sect wanted me to renounce playing any computer games on the laptop, playing in the role-playing game clubs, even the love of travel. This blew me away because I thought Mormonism was strict with its Word of Wisdom Law of Health and the oaths and covenants that you make with God. This makes me weep and makes me so very sad because I believe that a religious spirit which can be found in any church including my strips people of liberty and a good life.

Be Careful to have a relationship with God, not a Religion!

I've just looked out my window today, and I see many different things. I see people having fun. Couples walking smiling and holding hands. I see people laughing. And I think that God intended us to have a good life. God is not for fun and pleasure. Now not to allow God to be mocked, he is Holy and wants us to begin to live for him.

Religion can be something very much damaging. It is a religion that I believe has damaged my psyche here of late. It's because of religion that I have sometimes lost joy in this life or wish I never existed. I'm beginning to analyze this today. Having a relationship with God is what he has wanted for us all along. Jesus Christ even started when he was living that he has called us friends. We are to cry out Abba Father, which is almost likened to the word Daddy!

It's about knowing them personally. Not about following ethical rules or sectarian commandments.

Now before you think that I'm saying we can live however we want to live, I want to come against that right now. God is holy, and he wants us to live for him. He wants us to live with him forever, and if we begin getting to know God, we know that we have to live a life of holiness even to be able to enjoy the presence of him via the Holy Ghost and to live with him forever.

But what I am trying to drive home is that salvation is not by those rules!

Salvation is not in what man has received from God. We also understand that salvation is of Grace that we receive from God. Furthermore, salvation is found when we become his friends, his disciples, his companions.

End of Churchianity! Embrace God!

We get so trapped in the trappings of the church that we forget what we're here for. Our existence places us here to have a personal relationship with God. We are here to enjoy life; he has come to give us life and that more abundantly. Heavenly Father has designed life with the good, the bad and the ugly to teach us different lessons to help without progression.

I beg of you, my brothers and sisters! People can act out a religion for many many years and come to find out that they had no relationship with God. We have to begin to look at how God has framed his relationship with us. He calls us his children. Think of how you communicate with your earthly fathers. Do you never talk to them? Sometimes we don't. But if your relationship is ideal you talk to him; you spend time with them, you listen to their counsel and advice.

The Family is a Framework of what Heaven and our Relationship with God are like.

Look at the words that the Bible uses to address us. We are called

- The Bride of Christ
- Children of God
- Joint Heirs with Christ Jesus
- Friends of Christ
- Disciples of Christ
- Saint
- Believer
- The Elect
- And More

And when you begin to look at the various words that are used to describe us we can start to frame how Christ and Heavenly Father views us. We begin to understand exactly what sort of relationship we are to have with God. Yes, we are slaves to God bought with a price (his blood). But we are so much more to God. When Christ used parables look at some of the ones he used. Like the prodigal son, etc. The father in that story is so happy when we come back to him he kisses our necks, throws a robe around us and a ring.

In Conclusion

God is not some great overlord of the universe who does not care for us. He says to cast our cares upon him because he cares for us! (1 Peter 5:7). How do we grow in our relationship with God? Through prayer and fasting, we come close to him and grow in his love. Through scripture study, we are guided and shown which way to go.

Chapter Thirty

I Can't Envision a Heavenly Father of Love that

I Can't Envision a Heavenly Father of Love that Fundamentalist Christianity Teaches

An Open Letter on Fundamentalist Christianity

Dear Friends,

I am writing this publically on my facebook so that folks can be clear and understand something. I am a man. I make mistakes, and as I said in a different post I feel I have the wrong parts of Captain Moroni, Peter, Paul, and others all rolled into one. My wife and I were going to resign our membership in the Church of Jesus Christ of Latter Day Saints, not because of unresolved sin or anything like that, but because we wrestled with some doctrinal issues.

The Wrestling Match of the Century

It has not been an easy wrestling match. Sometimes things happen that are great and inspire us to keep on going. And sometimes things people say or have said cause us to examine the religion we follow with some very severe eyeglasses picking apart things. I deal with emotional issues from time to time. My desire is and was to serve Jesus. I thought that by membership in the church I was consigning myself to hell.

Is Heavenly Father just a mean Judge who wants us to have no joy in life?

But what I've seen from the "Christian" church makes me flee to the Iron Rod and walking towards the tree of life. I am not perfect. I have many faults in life. But some of the things that they believe make me want no parts of their God. I can't envision a heavenly father who acts in that manner. My good friend who is also my religious leader in the church said something to me that has been whirling around my head.

A God who is love cannot be the same one that Fundamentalist Circles Preach On!

He, in essence, can't envision a God who is "love" doing the things they teach. And if that were God he'd want no part of him. God chose some very exact language in the bible in how he describes his relationship to us and our relationship with him. He calls us his children. He is our Heavenly Father.

What is our Heavenly Father like?

I began to wonder why he used the term father. It is because that's how he wants us to identify our relationship with him. We don't necessarily like our parents all the time. And sometimes our fathers have to be <u>**disciplinarians,**</u> and that hurts. But if we have good father's and that's what God is, Good. Then we have to know that he loves us.

Why he likened us to his children and him our "Abba" Father!

So why did he call us his children? Because he treats us as such. God is not some mythical being in the sky who needs our worship. He is WORTHY of our worship, and we should worship him. But he does not need mindless automatons who's job is just to worship him. He wants us to have families. He wants us to enjoy our spouses and relatives and friends. In life, he has promised that he came to give us an abundance of it. (John 10:10)

I Publically Renounce Error

On this blog I wrote an article, I titled "My Exodus From The Mormon Church." or "From Minister to Mormon to Minister." I am ashamed I wrote it. Consider this article my retraction speech. That's why I wrote this here. I originally was going to write it on Facebook. Believe me; I will still share this there. But I made the error here, and so my retraction should be here.

What I Learned in a Fundamentalist Prayer Meeting!

I went to a prayer meeting tonight online in like a skype room. The things that they wanted me to renounce during this prayer made me and my wife physically sick. I entertained the idea because as I've stated above, I want to follow Jesus. But this level of fundamentalism reminded me of some almost Al Qaida and ISIS type stuff.

I don't believe God takes things overboard!

Renouncing various forms of sex with my wife. Renouncing my role-playing games and all of my friends I met there. Renouncing dressing up for role-playing games. Renouncing various spirits which would not come out of me (mind you they were not there from the get-go) You cant cast out what you do not have. Wanting me to renounce spiritual experiences. I thought God wanted us to have spiritual experiences with him.

I Renounce What I had said before!

Pure insanity is what this call was all about. I renounce them! In all of my time in the Mormon church, that church has done nothing but support my family and me. They have done nothing but prayed for me. Visited me when I was sick. Support my desire to move forward in life and have that abundance of life.

In one meeting these Fundamentalist Christians have turned me completely off to their version of Christianity. Jesus Christ has called us joint heirs with him. (Romans 8:17) And he has called us his friends. This is the picture of God that makes the most sense to me. I have taken down any **website** I was affiliated with that may have had on it any error.

I Ask Your Forgiveness for Momentary Lapse in Judgement

I humbly ask you, my friends, to forgive me. I was wrong. I can admit when I am wrong. And I ask for your forgiveness. I am a man. I want to exhibit the good sides of Captain Moroni, Peter, Paul, and others I have named. I want to help folks find Jesus Christ. Fundamentalism is very dangerous, and we have to be careful of it in any form. And while we're quick to bad rep Fundamentalist Mormons or Muslims, Fundamentalist Christianity doctrines can be just as dangerous. I pray you all forgive me for my error.

Sincerely,

Kenneth Green

Chapter Thirty-One

Sticks and Stones. A Treatise on Bullying and

Sticks and Stones. A Treatise on Bullying and Teasing

"Sticks and stones may break my bones, but words will never hurt me." - Childhood Rhyme

Do words really hurt like sticks and stones?

I laugh when I think about the above sticks and stones rhyme because it's so untrue. We walk around in life thinking were the Teflon Don. But at the end of the day what we say can affect others. Life is far too short to be wasted in negativity. It is far too quick to hurt others with what we say. I know I am not innocent in this, I say bad things to people too. But this morning some hurtful words were spoken to me more damaging than any stick that has been thrown at me.

Some Words that hurt like sticks!

This morning some people on Facebook stated that I was a Dyke and a woman trying to be a man. I know that I have an effeminate voice reminiscent of a kid. I know that I have soft features and a baby face to boot. But when I say this know I am speaking the complete truth I am a man. I have always been male, and will always be a man. I have a health issue called growth hormone deficiency that causes me to both have younger features like a teen kid and a light voice because of the deficiency I did not develop a regular Adam's apple.

I want to encourage you to be kind to someone today! Think about all of the people you may have hurt via your tongue. And then think about all of the people that have hurt you. When you begin to be more considerate in how you treat others that good karma (or blessings as I call them) will return to you. Many of us are born with illnesses. Many of us don't feel that we look good. Those feelings of self-hatred or inadequacy are terrible to deal with. But then when negative words and stares are thrown our way it compounds the negative self-hatred we are already feeling. God has made us all in his image. Religion helps me feel comfort in my tribulation (Romans 5:3)

"And not only so, but we glory in tribulations also: knowing that tribulation worketh patience." - Romans 5:3 (KJV)

Enduring Trials Well

We all have to endure trials in this world. Life may be easier for some than the others. We all have to endure hardships. God knows exactly what he is doing. Through the enduring of tribulations, we are now developing patience and trust in him. Tribulations develop Godly character and strength. So if you're dealing with harsh self-hatred and feelings know that this is not how your father in heaven views you. You are so beautiful and amazing to him.

Speaking from experience!

So yes I got off on a tangent about how we feel in this world. It's easy enough to do so as I'm speaking through experience. However back on topic of sticks, stones, and words. I hope through my passionate expressions and outreach that you can know my heart. If I can convince just one person to be considerate in how they treat others and what you say then I call this a win.

Cultural Corner: Smoke Weed Every Day!

On today's segment about Culture, i want to talk about gentrification in the city of Denver. I am proud to say that I was born and raised in the mile high city. When I grew up, it seemed to be half the size that it is now. Every since the Marijuana legalization took place this city has experienced a boom like the gold rush. But instead of mining for gold, people are clipping those greens.

Smoking weed?

I am not personally against Marijuana. I feel that if it helps you, Mozel Tov! Keep living! But what I do hate is living with this population growth that weed has sparked. Housing has reached all new astronomical levels in price and a sheer number of developments. Changes can be seen from the grocery store to schools. I love that Denver is growing and don't get me wrong I'm not against that. However, i would like to see the city slow down its growth rate.

Has the Green Industry helped Denver?

The Green industry has brought jobs, that is true.
But even the jobs that weed has brought are not available to the poor because of criminal records etc. The dope boy on the corner made some mistakes and tried to work and ends up with criminal records. Then are shut out of

the city for what they did. Marijuana has made Denver grow way faster than it should have. I hope that it slows down a bit to allow the citizenry to help shape the changes in our neighborhoods. It is so sad that whole communities are shutting people out who formerly lived there. I hope that we can make these positive changes.

Thank you for your time!

I want to thank everyone for taking the time to read our web page. We're hoping to make some huge strides in the coming days. I thank you for all you do, and if you reside in Denver why don't you let me know your thoughts about the fast-growing industry of Marijuana in the mile high city!

What would you like me to report on in the coming days? I want to start a series on a hard-hitting topic, but I am low on ideas. I thought a series on polyamory and the religious context would be interesting, yes polyamory not polygamy.

Chapter Thirty-Two

Going Deeper in the Word

Going Deeper in the Word

This week's study in the Word.

This week has been very interesting for me. It seems I am a yo-yo sometimes. Being a believer in Yeshua means that you have a desire to study the word of God. When I say the word let me be exact and definite, I mean the Bible. My favorite version is the Amplified Bible, studying with Logos Christian Software helps me in conjunction with the Amplified Bible to go deeper in my bible studies. I have been in the book of John lately especially the sixth chapter. A friend of mine who is not a Mormon suggested I read that chapter to ascertain the nature of God. And so I pulled out my tablet, and I began to dig.

Going deeper in the word than face value!

The things that I began to find via the Logos software allows me to understand the Greek that was being used in the New Testament. This is called Exegeting the word of God. I find this practice completely absent in the Church of Jesus Christ of Latter-Day Saints. They exhort you to read the scriptures daily, and I know there are some scholars in the church that are contrary to the rule. But the average every day Mormon will only read the scriptures at face value, and even then they state that the Book of Mormon is the most correct book on earth which I find to be funny. The Bible which covers thousands of years of confirmed history is said to be full of fallacies. I am beginning to take real offense at that notion.

Being Backslidden

The Church has become my life in essence. Most of my friends are members of this church. The activities that my wife and I go to are from the church. And the Lord has been dealing with me over the past two years about coming out of this. Two years ago when I had died, the Lord began to deal with me. I think the main reason I was allowed to come back to this earth after my death was because I was not ready for the judgment bar of Christ and God is so merciful. Woe to me, I feel so backslidden.

The work that Christ Jesus has begun in me; he is faithful and just to complete. When I began to look at the judgment standards for a prophet of God, the Lord began to deal with me in a mighty way. Joseph Smith Jr. by biblical accounts is not a prophet. If any of a prophet's words were not fulfilled, they used to stone them in the old testament. Joseph got shots from the gun instead.

Going off of feelings rather than the word...

The Church of Jesus Christ of Latter Day Saint's want you to believe something is fact via feelings in your bosom. This is a dangerous tactic that because we toss to the wind one of the most beautiful things that God has given us, our minds. The New Testament talks about these other gospels preached by angels. (Galatians 1:8) Makes me wonder why the Lord saw fit to include that in the Bible. Then we hear about all of these offshoots from apostolic creed Christianity that has been preached by angels. Makes me laugh when I think about this.

I know I am running on about this, but it's because I want to begin to explain my feelings via a biblical argument. The Lord has given us his word, which is his bible. The apostles did not try to alter the religion of the Savior. It is dangerous when modern-day prophets get "revelation" that is contrary to the Apostolic Creed.

I'm coming out!

Mormonism has great apologetics people who explain away their gospel. But all of the things they believe that are contrary to the Bible either originate from the Book of Mormon which was created via the use of divination tools supposedly called the Urim and Thummim, but in essence, it was Joseph tossing rocks in a hat that formed words. The Temple Ceremony almost copies word for word parts of Masonic rites. The Book of Mormon plagiarizes the Bible in several places almost word for word. Satan is very tricky and deceitful. He is a master of hiding the bad things amongst truth and twisting words.

The Temple Ceremony almost copies word for word parts of Masonic rites. The Book of Mormon plagiarizes the Bible in several places almost word for word. Satan is very tricky and deceitful. He is a master of hiding the bad things amongst truth and twisting words.

In Conclusion

I entreat you to do the research for yourself. Don't merely just read the words of the bible but dig deep into them. God bless you and keep you! I don't say these things to hurt any member of the Church of Jesus Christ of Latter-Day Saints but merely to educate and to hopefully cause a seed to be planted that will grow into deliverance from falsehoods and liberty in Christ Jesus! - Kenny

A Blast from the Past Blog Post!

Chapter Thirty-Three

Why is it hard to picture ourselves as children

Why is it hard to picture ourselves as children of divinity?

Are we children of divinity?

One of the simplest truths that I love my church teaches that is that were all literal children of God. We as humans short ourselves so much; we think we could not possibly be children of divinity. This has been a concept that has been challenging to me as I reflect on the doctrines of salvation. In the religious belief system, we are the literal children of divinity made with a purpose. And if we keep our covenants and do all that we are supposed to do then we can inherit all that he has including the ability to progress and evolve forever.

The Human condition hinders our vision of divinity!

Frailty is the destroyer of potential. When we live our life, we are in a human state. We do not have any characteristics of deity native in us from birth. But we can be born with afflictions because of our human frailties. And it's because of those that we lose sight of our potential. That is the saddest thing to me is losing sight of what the result of our lives is to become. We find divine power when we trust in the message of Jesus Christ. Faith in him, the divine one activates divinity in us. When we have confidence in his grace and atonement, and we apply that to our lives God has said that there is nothing that we can't ask for that he won't give. That does not necessarily mean we will get it in this life, but we will get it!

And I say unto you, Ask, and it shall be given you; seek, and ye shall find; knock, and it shall be opened unto you" - Luke 11:9

Divinity as an expression of love!

To me, this is where divinity comes from. One of my favorite hymns of all time is "I Stand All Amazed." To me, I do stand amazed because God is love. And I don't get where people think of this lofty God that is not involved in our lives or wants a bunch of minions just to do what he says and be in servitude forever. Mind you I don't mind being his servant forever because I am a dirty rag and am no good, and its only because of his love and grace that I have a chance to be with him. But am I deserving of that honor? No, I am not deserving of the privilege. And when I think about things in that light I am amazed

"I Stand All Amazed at the Love Jesus Offers Me." -I Stand All Amazed Hymn

God is the epitome of love. He is Love. And because of who he is I am so grateful that he does not act like the grand poobah Overlord from space that wants me to be his drone forever. But he wants us all to become like him. I respect my protestant brother's beliefs. But I am starting to fall in love with the doctrines of the Church of Jesus Christ of Latter-Day Saints.

Updates on my life!

I am sorry that I have not written much over the past month. To be honest I have had to deal with illness plaguing my household. Also, I told you that I had surgery on both feet, and as of late I have been diagnosed with Renal Cell Carcinoma. So I took a short sabbatical from blogging. But I want to thank my awesome readers who are still rocking with me. I love you all. I hope that I can inspire you to esteem yourself better than you are now. Now pride goeth before a fall, I don't want folks to get prideful because they are children of divinity. For pride is what caused Lucifer to fall and become Satan. But I want to encourage you to begin exercising your faith!

Chapter Thirty-Four

Genie In a Bottle Christianity

Genie In a Bottle Christianity

Random Blog Post by Kenneth Green

As I think about my life this past year all of the up's and downs of life, the trials and adversity. I reflect on how I think about God right now. I've had plenty of shouting matches at God. Asking my father in heaven "Why did you allow this?" I've also been guilty of "I don't want to believe in you because you don't want to help me." Famously the one I think of the most is the "Where are you!!!!" Trust me I'm writing this blog post as much as a reminder to myself in the future (hello numskull!) as I am hoping that it will help you.

Storms and The Sunshine!

Today I have been having some more issues. The day started with great news, the cast came off, and now I just have to wear two boots 24/7, and even though I've had to deal with that (which is better than a cast) it is surprising news! Then I had a bad argument with a friend who faked like he wanted to do something, then I fronted the cash for him to do that thing only to find out that he doesn't really want to do it. Friends always come with the real talk when you're dealing with others, please! It could save strain on friendships.

Why do we expect divinity to be like the fairy godmother or genie?

So from that point of having a shouting match with a friend I did what I usually do best when depressed, sleep. I woke up when I remembered a friend wanted me to fix a networking problem and words she stated to me always rang through that I could use her printer. So I went up to her house and fixed her printer and networking issues and in turn not only did she let me print off my character sheets for this convention which is a lot of printing (like 45 sheets of paper) and we talked about what's been going on in my life.

He is not a genie!

This friend saw me in my need. She is loaning me a wheelchair for the weekend, so I don't have to stand around for the convention which is awesome! This friend of mine is also providing me a ride to the conference hotel which is in the boonies. Even though I wanted to check in today to the con and hang at the hotel with friends from the club, i did not see God at work by the delay of not getting to go today I got my sheets done, got a wheelchair for the convention which will make things WAY better and I got the ride.

God works through people!

I am so grateful for the friends I have in my life. First I want to thank my business partner Brandon Murphy without whom this weekend would not even be possible. I want to thank my wife for caring for me even though she had a pretty bad day herself. I want to thank Mike Torrey my friend in the club who volunteered to give me a ride even though he's running security for the con. And last but not least I want to thank Sanddy, my friend who is giving me a ride to the hotel tomorrow with the loaner chair she loaned me so I can have an easier time at the convention.

The Conclusion

Sometimes we get mad at God because we expect life to go a certain way. I feel we also get upset at God because we compare our lives to others and get upset because we consider God should have done something different for us. God is not a **GENIE**! He is more like a fairy godmother who wants to help us!

Right View Points

But our lives are affected more by decisions we make! It's also affected by the choices that we make and that others make. And if you can't find the fault, chalk it to a fallen world. said it. Coming off real as I can be. Sometimes things just are not meant to go our way because the world is not right. It's not God's fault. He will come to our aid and help us faster than we can count. And I know for certain he cares for us. But we have to frame our relationship in the best viewpoint! If we do that we will have a better life and better relationship with him!

My Last Post! In Memory of John!

Chapter Thirty-Five

Positivity 101: Overcoming lies about ourselves!

Positivity 101: Overcoming lies about ourselves!

We tell the most lies to ourselves!

Over the next few weeks, I will be doing a series on being positive and how to maintain that. The past few weeks have been very hard for me and my family. We have had to overcome much adversity with a variety of issues. I almost liken myself to JOB of the bible. I feel sometimes that the things we have had to go through or are going through are too much or not our fault. But this is not true. Some of the things that happen to us are our fault. Also with how this world is, in it's fallen state some of the things that happen are simply because we live in a fallen world.

All Things Work Together for Good!

So now I have to evaluate how to maintain a right attitude in the midst of the storms. It is easier said than done. Believe me! If you could only see my personal social media you would understand my own struggles. I don't need to rehash them here, however, I will not state that this blog post comes from an outside perspective. So I began thinking about how I can turn the bad things that have happened to me for good. For I believe that even the bad things that happen in life can result in good for us. Romans 8:28 that "All Things Work Together for Good for those who love him and have been called according to his purpose." ALL things work together for good. Not some things, not just the good things, but ALL things.

The War we fight with the lies!

So for the first day in this weekly series over the next month or two, I wanted to speak to the lies that get told in our ears. In my church we have a magazine called the Ensign which has a very powerful article in it by [Elder Larry R. Lawrence of the Seventy called "The War Goes On!"](#) and my friend Leon asked me to read this article today because it spoke to my situation. As I read this article I picked up on one of the key things that have been in effect on my life. The lies that the enemy of our souls (yes that old devil Satan) and also the lies that we tell ourselves from our minds and flesh.

We are our own worst enemy with the lies we tell ourselves!

Sometimes we blame the devil or give him way too much credit. Not to say that he does not have a part in it because I will not let that serpent off the hook. However, there are many times that we tell ourselves lies. No matter if it's the enemy of our souls or the flesh that is telling us lies we can overcome those lies by stating the truth. So we have to figure out who we are and the infinite possibilities that we each have.

We are the children of divinity!

We have the ability to progress and become smarter. As children of our divine parents, we have the ability to exhibit some of their traits and characteristics. Satan loves to tell us that we are nothing. He is willing to sell us on this idea. But what makes things even funnier is the lies that we tell ourselves. We are guilty of being our own worst enemy sometimes. And we have to begin to counteract that. So here is what I suggest we do for an initial assignment.

Homework to help you become more positive and combat the lies!

Look inwardly to your strengths and characteristics. Begin to write down the good things about you. Keep this list on your tablet, phone, email, somewhere you can access it on the fly. Then READ it when Satan or when your own mind tries to interject lies about yourself. Read the good things about yourself and remind yourself that you're not supposed to be perfect yet. That life is not over and as long as your drawing breath you have the ability to grow and evolve. Even after you stop drawing breath you will evolve until the day when you have reached your full potential!

Chapter Thirty-Six

Grind Time – Motivational Monday Blog Post

Grind Time – Motivational Monday Blog Post

What is your grind?

Everyone has skills that God has blessed them with. I call these skills the care packages from a loving father. The father which I refer to is our heavenly father. Believe in yourself today! God has given you skills no matter your educational level or cultural background. Finding those skills is usually what is so hard to do. Most people overlook the innate natural talents that lie inside of them. Many times these skills go dormant for long periods of time but I don't believe they go away. So if I can encourage you to do anything is to begin to take inventory of what your good at!

Everyone has a grind! Everyone has Talents!

When you evaluate your talents and skills you will begin to discover a few things that you're especially good at. Once you find these things know that these things are your "hustle" or what I coin your "hustle" anyways. Anyone can have a hustle. I don't use the negative connotations of the word. When I use the word Hustle I use it in the same vein that I would use the word Grind. Money is not the most important thing in the world. I think that we get too wrapped up in the financial trappings of this world.

Money can help your life!

But if I can keep it real, money does help you be able to accomplish things in life. A person from a documentary I saw called money "Go". I like that terminology. When you have money there is nothing that you can't do. You can be a blessing and help others. When you have financial resources you can give to charity and to church. This world does cost, and being self-sufficient can be a huge boon to your life. Not having to worry about where finances are coming from can alleviate a lot of stress. This is something that the Green family is working on, self-sufficiency. Being able to be a blessing to our church via tithes and offerings. Having the ability to travel and have the fun experiences in life. These things are important. So what's your hustle? Get up and go to work! Your future is waiting!!!

Last Week's Motivational Monday

Chapter Thirty-Seven

The Power of Decrees and Affirmations

The Power of Decrees and Affirmations

By Kenneth Green

In today's blog post I want to discuss what I call the Power of Decrees. I have been reading a book lately called Powerful Key's to Spiritual Sight by Michael Van Vlymen which is a very powerful book. You can get this book now as part of the Kindle Unlimited Program which I LOVE. This program allows you to borrow ten books at a time from the Kindle library and has many books on a variety of subjects. I have learned everything from picture taking with my professional camera to blogging all from that library. This book talks about faith and I wanted to highlight something from the word of God for today's Motivational Monday.

The Power of Creation is in the Tounge.

"Death and life are in the power of the tongue, and those who love it will eat its fruits." - Proverbs 18:21

Not just Words but actions!

The Preacher's homiletical goes even deeper on the subject which I love. It compares our tongue's words to our conduct. And it is that conduct that will feed us. Not talking only in a work sense but what we do has an effect on what we receive in life.

The Secret to Success

I am not one who believes in a bunch of new age mumbo-jumbo. However, I do believe in the Secret. The Secret is simply whatever we state, we receive. If we talk negatively we receive negatively. If we speak positively we receive the same. We must be careful what we say or what we claim. I tell my wife this all the time to never claim sickness. I don't care what the doctors say, state that you are well. State that you are healed. Once you begin speaking positively then positive things will begin to happen. I have to remember that myself. God has given us creative power via our words.

The Power of Decrees in Our Life can Shape Our Lives!

We need to begin to practice gratitude for what we have already. From that place of gratitude, positive feelings will come. We must be careful what we say or do. Because if we claim illness or negative things and we don't send a reverse signal quickly those things will happen. I can't count how many times I've been sick and said to myself "I'm going to be admitted to the hospital" and I was! But times when I stated that I was well or that I was alright and would be going home, the same happened.

Be Careful how you use the power of decrees!

We have the power of Decrees in our life. We are children of the King of Kings. Whatever we speak with our mouth has the ability to come to pass. Perry Stone and Sid Roth stated something in the new year which I believe. I believe that in 2017 things we state will come to pass at such an astoundingly quick rate. We need to learn to be silent sometimes and when to speak. We need to know what to speak. I have faith that if you use this power well then you can unlock any blessing in the universe. Anything that you want can be yours.

The Universe will start to line up with what you have decreed and brought those things to pass. Be careful what you say, it can help and harm you!

Here is Last Week's Motivational Monday! Be blessed and I look forward to bringing you a new topic next week. Remember this week to be grateful and think positive and positive things will happen in your life! Take care!

Chapter Thirty-Eight

Decree's and Affirmations Whatever Friday Blog

Decree's and Affirmations

Whatever Friday Blog Post

Decrees and Affirmations Part Two!

Welcome to Friday fun day. This past motivation Monday I talked about affirmations. Now I want to give you tools on how to build your own affirmations, and a few decrees that I have made myself. The biggest thing that you must remember is faith in what you're saying. If you have faith in what you're saying then it is more likely to come to pass at a more rapid rate. However, if you do not believe then while the secret may continue to work for you, it will take longer and not bring the results desired. Faith is a leading part of the law of decrees. So let's get into it, shall we?

Putting the Law to work!

Affirmations don't work if you say them once and never pay attention to them again. To begin to put the secret to work for you, you must repeat the affirmations often. I like using time in the morning to say affirmations the prayers to help get my day started. I like standing in the mirror when I say them, this is not necessary however, I think it helps the affirmation get into your mind if you're looking at yourself while saying it. The first thing that you have to do when making decrees and affirmations is decided what you want in life.

Step One for Affirmations and Decrees - Visualization and basic planning.

Deciding what your life should look like is the first part of making decrees and affirmations. Begin with self-visualization of where you want to be in three months, six months and a year time. Doing t will help your affirmations become more real to you. Don't worry about making plans on how to get your goals at this juncture. That will come later, as you begin to see how to make your goals come to pass. Once you have an idea of where you want to go, begin to craft affirmations that match your goals. For instance, if my goal is to be debt-free in one years time I may design the following affirmation.

"I am debt free.."

"My debts are paid and clear!"

"I will be debt free by "

It's Okay to Be Afraid of Your Goals!

One thing that almost to set up as a rule right now is not to be afraid of your goals. If they are not scary the goal is not big enough! Remember, the God of the universe is the one helping you accomplish these things. The same God who created the earth in seven days destroyed it in forty and accomplished so many obstacles in his word. Once you have two or three goals for each time period begin to craft your affirmations.

In Conclusion

In closing these goals can be an area that you choose. I like choosing goals in the areas of finance, family, and with God. Having affirmations firing on all cylinders for those three areas that I am more organized and coherent. Somehow, I feel more connected to my purpose. Goals should be something fun, and again if they don't scare you a bit then they are not big enough.

One Last Note - There's nothing wrong with the scale!

You also must remember to scale your affirmations for the time frame your currently involved with. While it's good to have affirmations for the year time frame, the ones for the three months and six months are said more and are on my brain more because of the rapidity of when I want them to come to pass. I'm hoping to do this with my wife and get her to make her own affirmations. Share them with someone! This will keep your accountable for saying them! If your able to do this I promise that you will take the first steps into shaping your life how you want it.

My Original Post on Affirmations and Decrees

Chapter Thirty-Nine

As Wise as Serpents | Friday Fun Day!

As Wise as Serpents | FridayFun Day!

Being Wise

This week I've been thinking a lot about my spiritual gifts, and I have been pursuing the gift of prophecy. As I have been reading various books on the prophetic, I have begun to hear the Lord's voice via revelation. The Lord brought this verse to my recollection. I began to research and break apart this picture, the Lord's challenge and commission to the twelve. I hear a lot of preachers use this verse as causes belli to do some despicable things. Yes, Satan appeared in the garden of Eden as a serpent. But this verse does not give us permission to be underhanded in any way. This verse elaborates on how an apostle of the Lord should conduct themselves.

Breaking Down the Type of Wise in the Verse

The Greek word used in the new testament in this verse is phronimos which is pronounced from'-ee-mos. This word occurs fourteen times in the King James Translation of the Bible. This word can be defined in the sense that wisdom it denotes implies a cautious or discreet character. Wisdom in the dictionary is defined as

Having or showing experience, knowledge,and good judgment:she seems kind and wise|a wise precaution.•responding sensibly or shrewdly to a particular situation:it would be

<u>wise to discuss the matter with the chairman of the committee</u>.•[predict.]having knowledge in a specified subject:<u>families wise in the way of hurricane survival</u>.

What is wisdom? What is being wise?

So, the wisdom denoted in the verse is being cautious. We as disciples of the Lord Jesus Christ are to be wise in being shrewd and cautious. This wisdom does not extend to worldly wisdom or I should say phronimos (the Greek word) does not denote a wisdom in worldly affairs but having discretion and even more so discernment. As I began to think about this verse and exegete it correctly I began to have a light turn on in my head. I began to think about how I've heard this verse quoted over the years. And the preachers that have quoted them. God wants us to be both meek and lowly but also wise and cautious.

Discernment and Wisdom

In life, I think the biggest gift one could receive from the father is discernment. It is the opening stages to the prophetic and seer gifts. One must be able to discern and understand what one sees before that person can see or hear it. Operating in the prophetic (not the Pathetic as one of my favorite Christian comedians would say) takes this gift as a pre-requisite. How can you know the voice of God without the gift of discernment?

What about that being Harmless part?

So, while we are to be wise as a serpent lets exegete the other side of the token and coin. We are to be as harmless as doves. The word Harmless used in this part of the text comes from the Greek word akeraios

Pronounced <u>ak-er'-ah-yos</u>. This word does not imply being stupid or letting anything ride. On the contrary, this word simply means innocent. Harmless and simple. This word is only found in the bible three times. Our conduct is to be innocent. We are described on one hand as more than conquerors and on the other as gentle lambs in the New Testament. Why the contradiction? I believe that we are to be bold as believers. We are to walk in faith and be strong in the Lord. However, we are to do these things only out of the best of motives. Have you checked your motives lately?

What are your motives?

I have undergone a situation where I could fly off the handle at someone. I could get super mad at them and do as Kanye would say "Go Ham..." and if you don't know what Ham means I'm not going to explain it to ya that was from back in the day when I had my club ministry. (Laughing out loud it's a joke. I'm just telling on myself) lol. But I had to check my motives. Instead of flying off the handle I had to be gentle and kind. Does that mean I'm a punk or going to be punked? Heaven forbid! But it does mean that before I attack someone else or do something underhanded at someone else that I had to check my own motives. Have you had your motives checked?

In Conclusion

Lastly, I want to share a bit from a commentary I like to use. This is from J.O. Davies "Sunrise on the Soul." In regard to the verse, I wanted to talk about today.

III. The conduct they were to pursue. (1) Whatever should betide them, they were to remember Him by whom they had been sent. (2) They were to be wise as serpents. The apostle of any movement needs the by no means ordinary combination of zeal and wisdom. (3) They were to be harmless as doves; their wisdom was to be used neither to hurt nor to unnecessarily annoy. Their only concern was to be both harmless and wise, beyond that they had nothing and they had all, for they had God.

<u>Wisdom</u> for the day!

Chapter Forty

A God Who Rejoices Over Us

A God Who Rejoices Over Us

Zephaniah 3:17 – "The Lord your God is with you, the Mighty Warrior who saves. He will take great delight in you; in his love, he will no longer rebuke you, but will rejoice over you with singing."

The God of the Universe Rejoices Over You!

Praise the Lord I am so grateful for today. You know life likes to throw challenges at us, but we serve a God who delights in us. As I attended embrace covenant church today I sat and listened as Pastor Te Ana Brown gave her motivational message to the church today. I can't believe in all the years of my biblical studies that I never read the book of Zephaniah before. This book in the Bible is so cool!

God Rejoices Over Israel

I believe that God chose Israel to be his people because as a nation they reflect all of us as human beings. Israel went through some messed up stuff! I always tell people that if they like Jerry Springer or Maury Povich to read the Old Testament. Israel went through some things in their history. These people were given the distinct honor of being God's people, and they messed it up at every turn.

These people would obey God and keep his commandments one minute and the next engage in the worship of false idols from the nations that surrounded them. One minute they would listen to the prophets, judges, and kings that God placed over them and the next they wanted to disobey.

Israel as a nation shows how man is!

Even though Israel was wishy-washy and very tumultuous, God still loved them. In Zephaniah chapter 3 verse 17 talks about first and foremost how God is with us and how he saves! God describes himself as a mighty warrior who saves. Let that sink in a second. The God of the entire universe is willing to go to war for you. Let that sink in, about how important you are to God! When I think about that and makes me glad. Most of my battles I brought upon myself. My own selfishness, my lies, my conniving ways and more are responsible for my own messes! But even though I create my own problems the God of heaven is still with me, and he is still a mighty warrior who saves.

God doesn't just fight our battles! He Rejoices Over Us!

But then the next words brought a smile to my face! It says he will take great delight in you and he will no longer rebuke you. And he will rejoice over you with singing. Pastor Evan Brown illustrated furthermore that the king of all glory would sing over us. God does not want us to follow him to lord over us as a cruel taskmaster. His desire is to see us happy and his desire is to see us succeed! What a mighty God we serve! We are so lucky that our God is like that. I think of so many religions in the way people serve their deity. When I think of Islam and the way Allah is described. I don't think people in Islam or other faiths serve a God who calls them

Our God Is Different!

I think of Islam and the way Allah is described. I don't think people in Islam or other faiths serve a God who calls them a friend. Jesus calls us his friends. Furthermore, I do not believe that other religions serve a God who came and died on the cross for their sins! God is so good! Are you glad that you serve a God who rejoices over us? A God who sings in the heavens over us?

What a Gracious God we Serve!

Who would not want to serve a God like that? I get excited when I think about how good God is. I considered it just an honor to serve him without knowing how he sings over me. But now that I read these verses it has given me a new understanding of my Abba father. He rejoices over me and I rejoice in him! We must begin to treat our salvation as a relational experience. God is the God of reconciliation. His whole mission is to reconcile us to himself. He does this because he loves us! God is love! I am so excited about the thought that God sings for me. I would say I can't wait to meet him, but the truth is as he lives inside me I meet him every day.

<u>What an awesome God we serve!</u>

Chapter Forty-One

Balance In Life

Balance In Life

A Different Motivational Monday

This motivational Monday is going to be a little bit different. Today I want to encourage you to find something in your life that brings you great joy. Having hobbies and activities enrich our life a hundredfold. When I sit around with nothing to do I begin to become depressed. However, when I have a purpose, I find life to be supremely enjoyable. So I'll even share some of my hobbies that I like to do. The newest one is extreme couponing. Have you ever seen the show on TLC? My cousin Mary got me interested in saving money when I shop at the store.

Clipping Coupons Brings Me Balance

It goes beyond just shopping at the store. There is the time that you have to clip the coupons. Then we must research sales happening at stores so we could get the most bang for our buck. Then there is the actual shopping which is a fun activity within itself. There are clubs and social groups that get together and buy racks of newspapers and clip them. Turning the tedious part of the activity into fun. I'm even wanting to teach a class at my apartment complex on extreme couponing. This activity takes up hours of my time and while tedious it has become a lot of fun. I am now even on forums trading coupons of things we don't use for things we use.

What activities do you like to do?

Just talking about this activity is a lot of fun to me. I take goofy pictures of the tedious part to make fun of it. What do you like to do? How many hobbies do you have? These things make life fun and enjoyable. It is important to be sociable. If you want friends the best advice I ever heard was to be a friend. I am so excited for my new hobby. I may even blog about it on Tuesdays and call it Thrifty Tuesday's. Is that something you would be interested in seeing?

What does Balance have to do with Motivation?

Why would I talk about hobbies on the day that is supposed to be dedicated to motivation? Because if we're ever going to achieve what we want to achieve in life we must have a balance. There must be order and balance in every area. If one area is out of whack the whole being is unstable. I think sometimes in this world we forget to have fun! We're always so on track with our dreams and passions or even vocation that we forget to have fun. All of my posts on motivational Monday have been serious in nature! I wanted to share a glimpse into what makes Kenny tick.

Balance and the Pursuit of Happiness!

Is couponing the only thing that I do for fun? No way, I love music, gourmet cooking, watching TLC "don't ask", and cuddling my wife. I know that if I don't have fun I can't be motivated to be the leader, educator, and businessman that I am. You must dedicate some of your time to the pursuit of happiness. For some making money is all there is. But for others pursuing fun things is all there is. What is wrong with both of those pictures? The man who pursues only money can work himself into an early grave never getting to enjoy the experiences of life. The man who simply lives for pleasure and never pursues a vocation finds that fun only lasts for a minute before it becomes meaningless. Balance in all things is the key!

In Closing

In conclusion, I want to say thank you for reading my blog! God bless you and keep you is my sincere prayer. May find a balance in every area of your life.

Chapter Forty-Two

Live in the Moment

Live in the Moment

Today's Friday Fun Day will not be that long. I have been taking my medication oxycodone which has made me extremely tired and extremely sleepy. But I want to bring to your recollection the little moments that we all have in our lives. Today my brother and sister took the wife out and me for food at a new restaurant we haven't been to. As we sat down, two couples who were married it was a very soft moment. Many laughs were to be had as wives mate up jokes about husbands, and we try to reply.

Focusing on Living in the Moment

It's moments like these that we should always remember. They are the best minutes of our lives. I don't know looking across the table at my darling wife I fell in love all over again. Reading some of what she wrote in her journal made me sad for the things that she had been through.

Living in the Now!

Look for little moments in your life. I could look for the big moments in my life, but it's never for certain that big moments are coming. We could look for the moments in our everyday lives. Has somebody ever done something unexpected and nice for you? Has anyone genuinely blessed your life by doing something for you at school or work? The Lord made us his conduits for service and love.

While he could come down in the flesh, he prefers to use us instead.

Create your own little moment!

Look for the little moments in life that you can be inspired by. Look for ways that you can have fun in little ways. We sometimes want to look for bigger things and ways to think about doing it big. But you can find a great way to enjoy your life by being present in the moment. Lock yourself into living in the now. Do not live in the future or future events.

In Conclusion

I hope this short blog post will inspire you. I hope it will get you thinking of ways to bless others. When we look outside ourselves and look for others to serve. As my friend, Brandon would say "when we look outside ourselves we become the hands of Christ."

Chapter Forty-Three

The Real Enemy is Within

The Real Enemy is Within

It's Motivational Monday, and today I was struggling to find a topic to talk about. And then I got an email from a very wise person. This person has been preaching on reclaiming your territory. Each one of us has a destiny that the Lord has set for us. However, through our decisions and mistakes, we sometimes stray from the destiny or promised land that each of us has our territory.

Take Back your Territory

In this email, she wrote about the enemy's that we all have to face when we're trying to enter our destiny or our promised land, and you would be surprised at the enemy she lists. Who do you think your biggest enemy is? Is it the world or being worldly? Maybe it's that old serpent Satan is the enemy of our souls after all right? I would say that our biggest enemy is ourselves!

We are our own worst enemy sometimes!

That's right ourselves. We cut our throat at times. You're asking me what I mean by that? I will tell you! Fear, doubt, depression, all these are enemies within ourselves. Reading this book Self-Deliverance Made Easy I have learned that our emotions are directly tied to our souls.

Don'tGive the Devil too much credit!

Satan is one person, and while he has minions, they are not attacking this every moment of the day sometimes. I think we give the devil too much credit. While we can defeat him and his demons we should start with the enemies we create ourselves. So how do we fight these inner enemies?

How do we fight the enemies within?

The first thing that we must do is evaluate ourselves. We must know fully what emotions are at work within us. Once we have an understanding of what is at work within us, we can move forward and begin tackling them one by one. Sheer will can defeat some of these enemies. Some will require prayer, Bible study, and fasting! Some require the help of others, people like therapists, close friends, and advisors.

In Conclusion

I am certain that once you start defeating the enemy's within you, you can see the bigger enemies that are outside forces people like Satan, his demons, and this fallen world. We have so many enemies that are within, and we don't have to wait for someone else to deliver us or set us free from these enemies. You should take more credit for who you are the children of the highest God! At least those who have a relationship with God are. God said greater is he within you than he in the world! You are more than a conqueror through Christ Jesus its time! Time to take your stuff back! Let's go to war if I could be praying for you in any area please email me at ken@simplykenneth.faith

Chapter Forty-Four

Holiness and Mercy

Holiness and Mercy

"To desire and expect nothing for oneself and to have profound sympathy for others is genuine holiness." - Ivan Turgenev

Family and Friends Friday Blog Post

It has been a very interesting week for me. Yeshua has been dealing with me on a great many different spiritual matters. I only want to please him with my life, my energies and my time. I am starting to understand my aunt and uncle the pastor and evangelist. As a kid, I don't believe that I was in love with Jesus as I am now. The more I draw unto him, the more in love I am. Reading the Bible and Christian books fill my attention and focus. When I was in the hospital, I felt very alone. Not saying that I was alone, only that I felt alone.

Thankful for my family and friends who were there!

In the more I had to lean on God, the more people failed me. Not saying that everyone did, my wife was there for me, her friends were there for me, my mentors the Fritsche family was there. And Pastor Brown was there. But people that I felt would have been there first let me down. I'm speaking of friends from the Mormon church. I was so used to them always being there for me that it caught me off guard. I needed prayer and could not get one single person to visit me. Now that I think about it when I first had heart failure only one person visited me from the church.

Holiness is now a life pursuit! It is now a lifestyle!

This experience has caused me to lean on Jesus for my support. And so I wanted to share some of my experience with all of you. Holiness by definition is the state of being holy. Holiness is something that we cannot perfect in life, but mercy allows us to return to God anyways. Holiness is something that is not prideful, not selfish, and not boastful. It is Christ-centered, Christ taught, and Christ-magnifying. The more I study the Bible, the closer I'm drawing to him. I mean following him in spirit and truth.

Warning: I'm coming against legalistic ritualistic belief systems now!

This may be a cause for alarm for some of you. But I find the Mormon faith to be legalistic in placing people under spiritual bondage that Christ died to free us from. It is highly ritualistic, legalistic in the commands you are to follow, and vastly different from biblical New Testament Christianity. I told you some of you might not like what I am writing today. But I promise that it is the truth as far as God has shown me.

Holiness in Conclusion!

So, the question is what do I do now? I know for a fact that I want to serve Yeshua in spirit and truth. I want to walk in his love, helping everyone that I meet. I want to give him glory via in my life. I don't care if he wanted me to clean churches all day. I want to serve him in spirit and truth. And so I have begun to walk as a born-again Christian! I will not be ashamed of the gospel of Jesus Christ, nor will I hide what he has taught me. I hope you still rock my blog's after reading this.

Chapter Forty-Five

Perceptions and Truth

Perceptions and Truth

Special Friday Blog Post

As I begin to think about this week I have a lot on my mind. I've been reading a book on unforgiveness. How dealing with it can unlock feelings of joy and peace in your life. The Lord does not only teach a lesson by using examiner as well. I'm starting to realize through a series of recurring dreams some areas in my psyche that had not fully been surrendered to the Lord. These areas have been brought to recollection especially since I've been dealing with my foot injury.

Our Minds The Playground of Satan

Satan loves to play our insecurities against each other. One of the Biggest I've dealt with in life is the fact that I can't make it on my own. As a child, my great aunt instilled a lot of this in me. Having been told that I'm slower than everyone else. Here lately I've been having dreams of a time when I lived with my aunt and uncle. Being afraid to disappoint my uncle, or being disobedient even though I was an adult. Satan likes to make you think of the worst times in your life. For me, this was a pretty bad time in my life because I felt I could do more but feel unknowingly held back in life.

Perceptions are often different than truth!

I realize that people did what they did in trying to protect me. Though I think some of it was selfish. My perceptions and what is truth might be two different things. Satan loves to play on our perceptions.

per·cep·tion

pər'sepSH(ə)n/

noun

1. the ability to see, hear, or become aware of something through the senses.

"the normal limits to human perception"

2. the state of being or process of becoming aware of something through the senses.

"the perception of pain"

synonyms: recognition, awareness, consciousness, appreciation, realization, knowledge, grasp, understanding, comprehension, apprehension; formal cognizance

<u>"our perception of our own limitations"</u>

<u>3. a way of regarding, understanding, or interpreting something; a mental impression.</u>

<u>"Hollywood's perception of the tastes of the American public"</u>

<u>synonyms: impression, idea, conception, notion, thought, belief, judgment, estimation</u>

<u>"popular perceptions of old age"</u>

Perception at its core is dual.

Perception at its definition is dual. There are things that we see through the senses. And there are things that are ideas or impressions of things. I'm a believer that the enemy likes to play with both. But today I'm especially talking about the Latter. The enemy has been against me with thoughts that I would regress back to that life I had with my aunt and uncle. It's not that it was the most horrible like to have. But having been on my own for 10+ years, I think it's the loss of independence that has me worried.

And this illness has made me less independent of late. So Satan has used his ripe ground to plant fears and old memories. But when I think about God and everything he's brought me through he is more faithful to me through my mind gives him praise. He's been so good to me; others discounted me yet he believed in me. He brought people around me who believe in me, and support me. So thankful that I am having these dreams. I believe that the Lord has brought me to this to deal once and for all with these feelings. I've been talking a good game on this blog about forgiveness for a few months. God is making sure I put my money where my mouth is.

Altering my perceptions!

I don't believe they think they did anything wrong. And maybe they only did wrong in my perception. However, I know how much the Lord loves me. He has been so faithful to me that I can rest in him enough to let go of my feelings towards my family members who I feel have wronged me. So be careful what you write and talk about because sometimes life or the Lord will make you put your money where your mouth is. I am doing better, so much better. I'm home; I have a wife who loves me and getting better physically. I had genuine true friends who love and support me.

Love Me True Book Review

Part of why I am doing a special blog post today is to review a book. This book is called love me true by Jason Whiting of Cedar Fort Publishing. I love this book and a lot of times I get called upon to review books for various publishers. But as a new husband, I found this book especially valuable. This book deals with one of the most important subject matters in relationships, honesty. I like how it illustrates dishonest behavior in marriages and relationships. A lot of times when were dishonest it is not intentional or malicious.

Sometimes it is out of fear, or myriad of motives. I think this book should be read by all married couples within their first year of marriage. Having a foundation of honesty will ensure that a marriage lasts. But a lot of times people don't realize they are dishonest. I want to incorporate this book into family devotional time. So we can build a forever marriage. I give this book the highest ratings because it's not just about straightforward issues. There are a lot of issues I did not realize I had until reading this book. So check it out today!

Chapter Forty-Six

Trials Are Good For Us

Trials Are Good For Us

Trials are good for the soul! Trust me I know!

So as I begin This Day some blows and some defeats. I'm still in the hospital, but the hospital has taken phenomenal care of me. Sometimes the enemy comes to try and make me feel sad because I'm here. Or make me feel sad because of the road to recovery that I must walk down. Next week I was supposed to travel to Salt Lake City for the biggest genealogy convention in life. As a member of the press, I would have been able to interview stars, have unprecedented access to the event a network with some of the best.

Disappointment Is a part of Life!

But because of my illness that I'm facing right now, I cannot go. Part of me wants to cry. Because I finally feel that I have achieved the status I wanted in my career. But as I think of how good the Lord has been to me I know that bigger things are coming. Before I would have let this destroy me. I would lash out at family and friends. I would be a real jerk. And from time to time I still feel that way. It's easy to think that way.

Doubts, Fears, and Doubts

Even right this second have my doubts. Sometimes the enemy of my soul knows how to fight the best. He fights on the battlefield of the mind. He likes to cause us to play on our deepest fears. It is a war that is constantly being waged. I must admit that it's easy to lose. So many people lose this war every day. I almost feel like a prisoner to my illness. I've been bedridden for the better part of a week. I have to have assistance just to get up to use the restroom. It makes you want to cry.

Loneliness and Trials

It's easy to feel alone. Being in a hospital room by myself is very lonely. Nurses and staff try to help you feel differently. But it's still a very lonely place. I miss home, I miss my mother, I miss my cats, but most importantly I miss my wife. This trial is just about as bad as when I had heart failure. If it were not for the Lord on my side, I would wallow in despair. So what have I learned from all this? The first thing I learned is that everything is not always as it appears. Yeshua gives Godly discernment in all situations. It is best to lean on him and never yourself.

I learned that health is something to be treasured. You can lose it at any time. True friends and family will always stick close to you during trials and adversity. Fake friends will become apparent just as fast as your real ones. Only these things can be learned in the trial. When everything is going good in your life, these things are harder to see. Trials give you experience. I do want to give you some notes to think about during the trials.

1. Things often are not as they appear. Take your time before making any decisions or rash judgments. Solomon was not the wisest man because he decided to split the baby into pieces. He was the wisest

because he saw the situation from all sides and made judgments accordingly.

2. Know that if God brought you to it, he could bring you through it. As long as you're alive, it's not over for you. As long as you draw breath, you have a chance to overcome. It's not the easiest advice or even the easiest to say. But this is something I'm learning with bitter tears.

3. Last but not least don't be afraid to lean on Yeshua. Part of his sacrifice in the atonement was to teach him how to suffer. He did this willingly to learn how to succor us. Because of this understanding, you can rest assured he understands what we're going through.

Chapter Forty-Seven

Amazing Ways to Overcome Our Defeatist Attitudes

Amazing Ways to Overcome Our Defeatist Attitudes

"Being a defeatist is evidence of you believing the lies of Satan about you." - Dr. Kenneth Green, D.D.

2 Timothy 1:7 - "For God hath not given us the spirit of fear; but of power, and of love, and of a sound mind."

We can overcome our defeatist attitudes! Today I write my motivational Monday blog post from a place of pain. Much as happened to my family and me over the past week. God lives and loves each and every one of us. We are born with such great potential that it's a shame how much we waste it. Today I was thinking about finances and affording my trip to Salt Lake City. This trip could change my life reporting for major Denver newspaper. But it seems like the devil wants to block all my blessings.

Lies of the Devil

And part of me started to buy into the lie of the devil. You will never raise enough money, you can't afford this trip, and nobody cares that you're reporting for the newspaper. These are some of the lies that the enemy is placed in my head today. But as I think on the verses me and my wife studied the other night from the Holy Bible I know that my God shall supply all my needs according to his riches in glory. Philippians 4:13

Lies about us come from one source!

My God shall supply. He promised me as a child that my gift shall make room for me and take me before great men. What an amazing promise. But these do not just promise me; they applied to every believer. So if my God who is not like a man that he should lie, why would his word lie to me? It is simply not so. God does not lie, but Satan does. God's word states that Satan is the father of all lies. Every lie that we buy about ourselves can be found coming from one source.

Being a defeatist is evidence of you believing the lies of Satan.

When we take defeatist attitudes, we are buying into lies. It's easy to do because sometimes the truth is too hard to take. We talk about ourselves sometimes the truth is especially hard to buy. Yeshua promises us that as we believe in him, we become joint heirs with him. You have believed a lie about yourself for far too long. How much longer are you going to deny yourself of positivity? How much longer will you defeat yourself before you begin?

While some Christians may say, I'm about to blaspheme I will say this. I believe in the secret. I believe what we say out of our mouth can have a direct effect on events that happen in our life. This principle is even biblical; the Bible states that the power of life and death is on the tongue. Why do you think Satan lies to us so much? Because we begin to believe it and then out of our mouth we restate the lie. Once we do this, we speak it into existence, and a lie becomes a reality.

How to overcome our defeatist attitudes?

So what can we do? How can we overcome our defeatist attitudes?

Step one, bind everything that enters your mind that changes your emotional state to negative outlooks. Step two reinforce yourself by reading God's word and positive motivational writings. Step three when negative lies enter your mind combat them with God's word and the positive things that you read. Lastly, spend time in God's word and prayer. As you get to know him, he will help you get to know yourself, and once you know yourself, you will be less apt to believe the lies of the enemy.

Examples of using God's word as affirmations...

Here are some affirmations that I use myself.

"For my God shall supply all your needs according to your riches in glory."

"You are more than a conqueror through Christ Jesus."

"All things work together for good for those who love the Lord and who are called according to his purpose."

"And your gift shall make room for you and take you before great men."

"You can do all things through Christ Jesus who strengthens you."

"And God has said, for I know the plans I have for you says the Lord they are good and not of evil to give you hope and a future."

"Forgot has not given me a spirit of fear but of power and of love and of a sound mind."

Our birthright as conquerors!

I hope the Scriptures that I have turned into affirmations give you strength and the ability to know who you are in God's eyes. I'm not here to sugarcoat things because life is hard. God allows us to live in a fallen world.

And because we live in this fallen world we have to deal with trials. A lot of the times we bring the trials upon ourselves. And then we want to blame others. Even though all these things you are still more than a conqueror.

I was watching the Morgan Freeman show called the story of God. This show talked about chosen people who lead others to God. These persons accomplish supernatural things. I believe this is because the supernatural world is real. More real than our natural world. The supernatural works both ways. I believe that Yeshua is the only way to God. But we have an enemy that empowers others of different beliefs to accomplish the supernatural. We have the same ability if not more being the children of God. It is up to us to find our birthright. Not until we find who we are will we ever even come close to some of the things that humans can do.

In Closing

I hope you've enjoyed this motivational Monday. Don't get it twisted I'm not a guru. I'm nowhere near perfect. My purpose in life is the point to God. When I overcome, it is because of God. Because of who God made me to be, not because of ability, and not by luck. I'm only God's servant who was not fit even to wash his feet. However, I would with my tears of gratitude for who he may need to be. God bless!

Last Week's Motivational Monday - Blessed are the Peacemakers

Chapter Forty-Eight

Unforgiveness, Just Let It Go!

Unforgiveness, Just Let It Go!

"To live with unforgiveness is to become a captive cultured citizen whose taxation is that of demonically ticketed torment." - Tracey Bond, Spirit Fed Entrepreneur: Growing Your Business with a Fearless Mindset

Jesus saith unto him, "I say not unto thee, Until seven times: but, Until seventy times seven." - Matthew 18:22

Unforgiveness and this Website!

Welcome to the inaugural post of the simply Kenneth website. Today I want to talk about forgiveness. I've been reading a book called self-deliverance made simple, and it has changed my life. It talks about the power of forgiveness. Jesus Christ taught that we should forgive seventy times seven. He was not speaking to give you an exact number but to show the magnitude of which we are to forgive. The reason why I chose to talk about this is that I am grateful and sincerely appreciative that I got hacked yesterday.

Being Hurt

Being hacked destroyed work that I put in over a year for on my online positivity website. I'm grateful that at least the work I've done on genealogy gangster will be saved. I could harbor many feelings in my heart right now. It would be easy to keep unforgiveness for those persons. I'm not perfect far from it, but I don't know who I've offended in such a way to cause my websites to get hacked. I don't even know who did it it would be so easy to harbor unforgiveness. Forgiveness is not something for the other person. It is something for you when you harbor and hold on to unforgiveness you're hurting yourself.

Unforgiveness Just Hurts Us!

Many times people don't even know that you're holding feelings of anger or unforgiveness against them. Tyler Perry as his classic persona Madea stated in the movie Madea Goes To Jail how others are living their life, and you're still harboring unforgiveness. Isn't that funny? Unforgiveness invites demonic activity to reign over your life. Demonic hitchhikers love it when you're feeling emotions of anger, hatred, and unforgiveness.

Taking Steps To Alleviate Unforgiveness

It has been proven scientifically how unresolved anger affects the body. Unforgiveness only hurts you, and worse it only hurts your soul. We can release these feelings by engaging in prayer. Closing our eyes and worshiping God. Then thinking about what happened and how it made you feel. And then at that moment asking for prayer that one died for all our sins help you to forgive.

Sincerity is most important!

It must be sincere. No one will care what you do because this is something that is mostly internal. You have to mean it from your heart. You have to mean it from your soul. However, once you forgive and learn this practice for every situation in life, you will find forgiveness for your sins. You will find healing in your soul. And most importantly you will find peace.

Finding The Good!

Finding the good things in bad circumstances will have tons of positive effects for you. Blood pressure, heart pressure, and many other illnesses can come from feelings of harsh anger. When we are set in our ways and refusing to forgive or to let things go, we hurt ourselves not just physically but spiritually. I am a believer that when you hate someone else, you are only hurting yourself. I think Buddha had it right in that when we are concerned with the happiness of others, we can find the ultimate happiness in ourselves. And when we are only concerned about our own happiness we are causing ourselves the ultimate harm.

No It's Not Easy!

These qualities are not easily obtained. Even right this moment I am angry over what happened to me. I will not hide that I even shed tears because I felt the attack was personal. And I don't know who I wounded so badly to do this. However, one thing I do know is that my God is greater than the world. And he who lives in me is greater than the world. So we can focus on this great new site which I'm highly impressed by how it looks and be grateful because I would never have created this site if my old one had not been under a hack attack I look forward to sharing what's on my mind on this website.

Chapter Forty-Nine

Bootstraps

Bootstraps

Why is Kenny always talking about Bootstraps?

Why do I talk about bootstraps so much? Life has a way of kicking everyone in the teeth. I don't know how many times I have to reiterate this message. I have been having the year from hell. Yes, I cursed. Sorry, don't get it twisted i've been saved all day and no sin has entered my heart. But life has kicked me and my family while were down. I hope that your not a complainer. Because if you are i say move over let me share some complaints with you for a few minutes.

    This year has been one of extreme testing. I have had a foot condition that caused me to be in the hospital for over a week. And then off of my feet for the most part for the past six weeks. Our family lost a member of our family. And before you get it twisted I mean child. Yeah, I know what it's like to lose a child. On top of that as if that were not bad enough I had to miss the convention I had been looking forward to for months because of this foot injury.

    If you think you got hold of this I got more!

    Okay so now you may say that's nothing. Well, let's go even deeper. Last Saturday my wife was impounded. The year her car was impounded. As if I could trip on that they say that it was a **HIT AND RUN** are you getting the picture yet? So she may have to face charge when she never hit anyone, And if you think you got a handle on this let's go even worse, she lost her job this past week. Get the picture more clearly?

Coup d'grace

And today I woke up to four hundred dollars missing from our bank account. Yeah, I have dealt with so much over the past few weeks. And I wanted to crawl into bed and stay there. I cried yeah, this is true. But then I got angry. I got up and said to myself, that if I stay in bed I will never have nothing. If I stay in bed our family will never have anything. And then our losses would be for nothing. So I pulled myself up by the bootstraps and I went to work. I could wallow, but who is going to feel sorry for me? Who is going to have pity? Yeshua (aka Jesus Christ) had to deal with so much and he never stayed down. So why should I?

Pulling myself up by the bootstrap!

So I'm moving on. I'm at work and I'm grinding. I'm making plans and I am figuring out things. I don't want nobody feeling sorry for me. Don't feel sorry for me because I don't feel sorry for myself. I am just fine. I am a bootstrapper. What is a bootstrapper?

<u>Bootstrapper Definition:</u> **1.**<u>(of a person or project) using one's own resources rather than external help.</u>

I love this definition. It's time that we stop whining as a society. Yes, life is hard, but it is hard for everyone. This is what I am starting to realize, No one on this earth has it easy and that's because of its a fallen world. Satan is in control of everything. And no matter what we think life does not owe us anything. There is a bible verse that comes to mind today and I want to share it with you all.

Matthew 11:12 " And from the days of John the Baptist until now the kingdom of heaven suffereth violence, **and the violent take it by force.**"

Lessons from the Violent

So what does the end of that verse mean? I know what the beginning means, It's quite simple. The Kingdom of Heaven is meant to endure. We are meant to suffer. John the Baptist was killed for something he never even did. He was killed because of a jealous woman. So in this verse, it talks about the characteristics of a disciple of Jesus Christ. But people forget the end part of this verse.

The violent take it by force. What did Jesus mean in this verse? I like to believe that we are to suffer violence. But we must not be afraid to take it by force. Sometimes God condones us pulling ourselves up by our bootstraps and taking it by force! God bless!

Last Week's Motivational Monday

Chapter Fifty

Darkest Before the Dawn

Darkest before the Dawn

This year has been one of the toughest of my life. I believe it is personally because of the positions I have taken on the internet. I am a believer in the secret and whatever you put out into the cosmos you get back. I believe this principle to be found even in the bible where the word says.

Proverbs 18:21 "Death and life are in the power of the tongue: and they that love it shall eat the fruit thereof."

I believe what we send out via what we speak we get back. On my blog, simply Kenneth I talk about being a peacemaker and in my life, I have been challenged to create peace. Basically, I believe that the cosmos is giving me the chance to put my money where my mouth is essentially. Be careful what you preach on because life and the cosmos will test you on it. Even yesterday I came under personal attack from the apartment complex where I live. I'm not going to give names of the place because God wants me to be a peacemaker. But I live in low-income housing as of the writing of this book and this place has its problems. I used to fight for this building as an activist. But lately, I've had a very isolationist stance. But the world is using this building to test my teachings and my beliefs.

This year I have dealt with a plethora of health issues. I began facing Kidney Failure and the very real possibility of kidney dialysis. As of this writing, I am not on dialysis. And I am now engaged in doing the best that I can to fight going on dialysis.

I've had to deal with a foot injury that has plagued us this year. My wife has had her own struggles as well and it has been very trying for our family. So now that I have begun this chapter by illustrating some of the troubles we are facing in 2017 its time for me to talk about what I wanted to get to which is that life is always darkest before the dawn.

What you send out as far as vibes and thoughts will return unto you. What you speak with your mouth can and will come to pass. I fight that battle of speaking positively all the time. It is the very tough thing to do. It is so easy to speak negatively and many times we do not even realize when we are doing it. This is very dangerous and tough to deal with. However, when we learn what we're doing we can begin to reverse the trend and work towards putting the right things into the universe. I am a believer that this year is going to be a huge tremendous blessing to me and my family. I believe that God is getting ready to show up and show out in our lives.

I believe this year has been so tough mainly because of what is getting ready to happen in our lives. I believe that God is getting ready to give us that Job type of blessing. Where our latter end is more blessed than our former state. Do you see what I'm doing in just this paragraph here? I am sending positivity (a word I've coined) into the world. I am sending good thoughts out over my year. I am so persuaded that I am using my tongue via my words on the page to decree blessings over my life.

It has been so dark because it is about to be dawn. In your life, it is sometimes the darkest points that transform your lives. I am about to be transparent here. I am not the best person in the world. I have had many failures in my life. I recognize this. And even though this chapter might not be the best place to put it I want to apologize to those I have not been good too. Now back to the subject. I believe that in our lives Satan attacks us right before the breakthrough. If he can get us to give up he wins. How many people have committed suicide before they walked into their breakthrough?

    My friend if your reading my words and are going through a tough time know that this is not the end. Romans 8:28 is the verse that always comes to mind when we're going through things in life. The verse simply states

Romans 8:28 "And we know that all things work together for good to them that love God, to them who are the called according to his purpose."

Even the bad things that happen in your life can be a building moment. I am here to state that even the bad things in your life are working together for your good. How can you say this Kenny? Well, let me illustrate. The bad things that happen in your life add to your story! They are a testimony to the greatness of God and what he has done for you. How he has brought you through life and how he has blessed your life. It is a testimony that will help others as they face the tough things in life. Those things are good. They also develop your faith and trust in God, as you must deal with life and all it brings you learn to rely upon God even when you don't see his providence in your life. I am especially learning this lesson right now.

You have things to look back on because this world is fallen. You will always have to face trials and issues. And when you face these things you can look back on your past trials and turmoil's and have victory. You can rest assured that the God that delivered you before will deliver you again!

So, apply that to your lives. Know that even in your dark times God is there. Also, believe that God is getting ready to use this situation for your good and for your future. I want to leave this chapter with one more verse from the bible that speaks to your future!

Jeremiah 29:11 - For I know the thoughts that I think toward you, saith the LORD, thoughts of peace, and not of evil, to give you an expected end.

Chapter Fifty-One

Speaking on Spirituality

Speaking on Spirituality

As I think about my own walk with God. A walk with God is something personal. When you walk with God it is a decision that you must make on your own. I'm beginning to have a very Latter-day Saint view on the divinity of man. As a born-again Christian in my youth I was taught that God was a far off. That he was something that we cannot possibly understand. His vastness is unfathomable to human beings. Latter Day Saints believe that we are the literal children of God. And having that godliness in our DNA allows us the opportunity to become like him.

That is something hard to grasp for me. I told you that I would be honest in my book and I mean it. Every day I look at myself and don't see any divinity in me. However, my humanistic views cause me to wonder the nature of God, how he communicates with man and our future postmortem. It is not an easy concept to grasp for me, mostly because I've been ingrained in Pentecostal theology from birth. Sometimes I wish I had been born into a Latter-day Saint family so that my upbringing would be different. Sometimes I wrestle with God over the fact that I had been born into struggle, strife, and adversity.

    Sometimes, the heavens are brass for my sake. I feel like I'm banging against the heavens asking for answers to prayers and receive none. I had been many religions in my life. I began my life as a Christian, brought up in a classical black Christian home. As I became an adult and had the freedom to choose for myself religion I have explored many including paganism, Wicca, Islam, Judaism,

Hinduism, Buddhism, and finally Mormonism. On my right arm, you will see a tattoo that invokes these religious symbols. I did not get it because I believe in a one world religion, but mostly to catalog my struggles on flesh with spirituality.

Even now as I write these words I am dealing with a debate on religion. I have people tear me apart in different directions. I have sought the heavens for help, and had not received the answers that I seek. This has planted a seed in me of doubt. However, I believe this time in my life is preparatory for me to receive my true calling in life which is to motivate and inspire others through my writing. I stand all amazed at the love that God offers me because I'm not always been faithful to him.

There were many times where I betrayed my sense of God. Many times, where I committed what my faith call sins. The more I live the more I understand the struggle in God's plan of happiness. I believe that our struggles have a purpose in our lives to help us be humble. I also believe that they help us stay connected and rooted in divinity. Lastly, I believe that they help us to see our own true potential. This is the point that I wanted to elaborate on and I know that I took a while to get here.

If Mormon theology is correct then we are the children of God. Each one of us has within us a divine spark, a connection with divinity. I find more in common with other religions each day and Mormonism. The fact that we believe that we have a heavenly father and a heavenly mother amazes me. Human society is both so why when not eternity be both? A lot of Judeo-Christian beliefs limit the role of women in society. My religion believes that women are valued and an essential key to eternal happiness. We are much more feminist then believed.

When I think of the eternities I don't think I could bear to be without Rachel. When I think of the life that we are building on this earth, it saddens me to hear the words till death do you part. I know the Judeo-Christian belief is that Christ fulfills all your needs on the other side. That you become his bride and therefore don't need familial relationships. But why would God have families in the first place if they were not valuable to us? I firmly believe that I will know my wife through the eternities. I also believe that if she chooses to be, she will be my wife through the eternities.

Elder Jeffrey R Holland stated it best," heaven without my wife would not be heaven for me". I believe that God made families be together forever. The relationships that we build on this earth have the potential to continue forever. We have the potential to develop love in families over the eternities. What a beautiful concept. And so, when I began to think about eternity in those parameters I began to understand God's plan for us. I also want to educate many of my non-Mormon friends on some of the beliefs of the church. We believe in religious freedom hardcore. While many may believe that we are strict in our beliefs if you read the teachings of Joseph Smith you understand differently.

In the articles of faith verse 11 it states, "We claim the privilege of worshiping Almighty God according to the dictates of our own conscience and allow all men the same privilege, let them worship how, where, or what they may". Look at that! Part of our very articles of faith states that we allow all men the same privilege. Articles of faith in case you don't know are the 13 guidelines or core beliefs of the church of Jesus Christ of Latter-Day Saints.

I am intrigued by the misconceptions that people have of Mormonism. Us Mormons have not done a very good job in combating the deception that is out there about our church. We can do better! I hope that my friends that read this book who know who I am can now understand better why I believe in the church of Jesus Christ Latter Day Saints. Are there things the church has done that I don't agree with? Plenty of things! But when I look at all religions and things people did in the name of God I give Mormonism a pass because all religions have done bad things in the name of God. We have done bad things in the name of God because we are human and we are fallen. I also believe we have done bad things in the name of God because of Satan who has deceived many.

And so, I want to end this by asking you to look into yourself. Every human need spiritualism. We all need to believe in something greater than ourselves. Look to yourself and find your own path. Would I like to baptize all of you into the church of Jesus Christ Latter Day Saints, sure! However, one of the blessings of Latter Day Saints theology that is unknown to many is that heavenly father's plan is there to save all. All unless you choose to be damned will be saved in heavenly father's plan. Whether you are Hindu, Muslim, Wiccan, or a member of the Church of Jesus Christ of Latter-day Saints. So, I challenge you to look up today!

Chapter Fifty-Two

Speaking on Spirituality Part Two

Spiritualism Part Two - The Addenda

I would like to let you in on my battle with my own spirituality. In the last chapter talked a lot about the various police systems that I have practiced over the years. I want to talk about that battle that is going on in my head, heart, soul, and spirit. Yes, I believe that each one of those things is distinctly separate entities that make up the whole man. Christianity has been pulling at me for some time. The Christian friends that I have all told me that Mormonism would be the cause of me busting hell wide-open. That is a very scary thought to me. I mean who wants to burn forever and ever in a lake of fire? Not this guy, I don't want to deal with adversity in my life and then die and go to hell!

I am like what James says about a double-minded man who is unstable in all his ways.

Because of this great battle between two religions, my thoughts are constantly flip-flopping worse than Mitt Romney. I don't want this to be, I want to follow my path for certain. But these small grains of doubt that have welled up with me have caused me to almost doubt Christianity. It has caused me to look at writings by atheist writers and agnostics and researching the history of the world in the scientific fact that we are older than several thousand years as the Bible promotes. Confusion is not of God. I know this for a fact! And I feel so confused right now. I promise you when I first wrote the very first pages of this book that we keep it real. And that's exactly what I'm doing.

I sat in a church service today, not my church but a small house church that operates in my apartment complex. It is led by a very good man of God who has done much for the kingdom sake. This man three years has come without pay a reward to minister to the low and downtrodden, the disabled and the elderly. I love this church, even as a latter-day St. I love the song sat facing and I love deeper into the Bible because theology is a passion. I sit and write this very confused because it feels like two belief systems are pulling at me. Mormonism gave me my independence and freedom, it to teach me what it is to be a husband and a man.

However, I am troubled that the gospel that they preach is so different from the gospel that Paul simply reiterates it first Corinthians 15. Paul's version of the gospel is very simple and states that salvation rests on that principle alone. The principle that Christ died, was buried, rose again on the third day, and was put in by many and ascended into heaven was the entirety of the gospel that was required to be saved. Temple ordinances, work for the dead, obedience to anything except the original good news that was preached by the apostles is all not included in what Paul was talking about.

There are many other things that cause concern for me with the church of Jesus Christ Latter Day Saints. I probably won't get this book published by the church of Jesus Christ Latter Day Saints because of the words I'm speaking in this chapter. But I would not be true to myself, and to you if I acted as if my beliefs were all sunshine and rainbows and no questions. It is not all sunshine and rainbows. I like many of you who are members of the church of Jesus Christ Latter Day Saints do struggle with the testimony of the gospel. My testimony is not struggling because of the actions of Joseph Smith, Brigham Young, or any other man. My testimony struggling because of doctrinal differences between the early Christian church and the church of Jesus Christ of Latter-day Saints. I'm not sure how this will all play out in • the end, or were how I will? All I know is as I'm writing this book you are getting a firsthand glimpse into my very hard and very soul. I want this book to tell my story, all the good, bad, and the ugly. I promise not to sugarcoat anything for you guys because I don't believe that you will experience victory or receive anything from my book if I am false to you.

Lesson: You are the Captain of your Soul!

As I think about a lesson for the end of this chapter I think about the poem Invictus. Especially the line where the poet states that he is the captain of his own soul. I have many people telling me what I should and should not believe. And it's a struggle that filtered through all the things that each side is saying to find the truth for me. Is cause many sleepless nights, much supplication and prayer to my heavenly father, much tears, and despair. As I think about my own spiritual journey in how to use Diane one thing I do realize is that the confusion comes from people. So, I am taking a step back and praying with my whole heart that I find what is right for me. Not what someone else says is right for me, but what I decide is right for me. You have free agency one of the most precious gifts given by loving God and creator. You can reason and think for yourself. It is not easy, as I am discovering right now. But it can be done! I am a true living witness of this fact. So, as you wake up and start your day tomorrow if you are lucky to do so remember you are the captain of your own soul. You can choose to steer it however you want. I believe I'm worse off than the captain of the Titanic so I'm choosing to allow Yeshua-Christ to be the captain of my soul today and every day. Who's the captain of your soul?

Chapter Fifty-Three

What's Next?

I don't know what is really next for my life. I don't know if you even read this works. I hope that my book is able to help people and to change lives. But I don't know I have no clue what God wants for my life or where God is taking me next. I pray to simply be used in his hands to be an instrument of his will. Just serve his people and his children. I hope that my words are able to enlighten strengthen and help people going through some of the same situations I went through. That is the weird thing about serving God sometimes we're flying by the seat of our pants. On social media, today Elder Nelson talked about the importance of prayer. And also the importance of the gift of discernment.

I want to speak on the latter the gift of discernment. Because it is the gift that will lead you to where God wants you. I believe that it is a spiritual gift that he desires all to receive. He wants all to know his will for their lives. He wants all to know what he wants them to do and what he expects of them to do. No, I believe in life we sometimes just go on Good Feeling. Or we go on what is in her brain. And I'm not saying that those two descriptors are not a part of discernment.

However what I am speaking to is a spiritual gift. Knowing the will of God is crucial for our lives. Without it, Satan can dragons too and fro. Not to say that God is not sovereign and cannot get us back on the right path. But not using discernment or not having discernment can cause us more heartache and more time than we need. That is what is next for me developing that gift and going on at the gift. Because I don't know how God is going to leave me. I have a vision of what I want for my life. And the types of experiences and things that I expect for my life. But that does not mean that that is what God wants. It could very well be what God wants but it may not be in the crucial thing for me and what is next is developing that gift of discernment. And figuring out what he wants of me. I believe that he is giving me a gift of leadership and I believe he is giving me the Gift of Gab for a reason. I hope to give firesides and go on the road with my book and help sell copies of my book and help change people's lives. And I read some of my heroes books like Al Fox Carraway and what she's had to do in her life and how she got her career going and I hope that God is leading me down the same sort of path. Public speaking writing more books being a good father a good husband a good friend a good Latter Day Saint. But I'm not sure what God's will is for my way I'm still serving a mission which is very important to me. And the fact that I want to finish that honorably May mean that I have to put my plans and designs on hold. Whatever is next for me know that I will continue blogging I will continue being a friend and I will continue being there for you God bless you God keep you and remember whatever God has for you next use discernment so that you may understand his will and go for it God bless you

<<<>>>

Made in the USA
Monee, IL
17 February 2021